JAN L. RICHARDSON

# In Wisdom's Path

*Discovering the Sacred in Every Season*

The Pilgrim Press
Cleveland, Ohio

The Pilgrim Press, Cleveland, Ohio 44115
www.pilgrimpress.com
Text and illustrations © 2000 by Jan L. Richardson

Printed in Hong Kong on acid-free paper

05 04 03 02 01 00   5 4 3 2 1

Library of Congress Cataloging-in-Publication Data

Richardson, Jan L.
    In wisdom's path / Jan L. Richardson.
      p.  cm.
    Includes bibliographical references.
    ISBN 0-8298-11324-1 (pbk. : alk. paper)
    1. Christian women—Prayer-books and devotions—English.
  2. Devotional calendars.   I. Title.

BV4844.R55   2000
242'.3—dc21

00-029836

# CONTENTS

*Illustrations*

Come to Wisdom with all your soul,

and keep her ways with all your might.

Search out and seek, and she will

become known to you,

and when you get hold of her,

do not let her go.

For at last you will find the rest she gives,

and she will be changed into joy for you.

—SIRACH 6:26–28


No language about God will ever be fully adequate

to the burning mystery which it signifies.

But a more inclusive way of speaking can come about

that bears the ancient wisdom with a new justice.

—ELIZABETH A. JOHNSON, SHE WHO IS


There is a pearl in every season. Find it.

Then give all you have to claim it.

—JOAN SAURO, C.S.J., WHOLE EARTH MEDITATION

# PROLOGUE: WISDOM IN EXILE

*I don't sacrifice animals to her.* I don't take secret oaths vowing allegiance to her. I haven't pledged my firstborn child to her or told anybody they were going to hell if they didn't believe in her. She is a big girl; she doesn't need this from me. She is secure enough in herself to know that people will seek her of their own longing and will honor her in their own ways.

She wears myriad disguises, most of which I will never know. But sometimes I glimpse her in the faces I encounter—dark, pale, wrinkled, smooth, laughing, weeping, aching, crying out for healing and peace.

She was there at the dawn of creation; she played and danced as the world unfolded. She is very good at amusing herself while the rest of us are busy debating so very seriously and arguing so hurtfully. She will weep while we tear each other to shreds, and then she will help tend the wounded on all sides. She will bite her tongue and refrain from calling us all the names we have called one another. She has a special place in her heart for fools; they will find a seat at her table and will eat of the feast and drink of the wine she has prepared.

I think of her now and then, imagine her biding her time with a cup of tea as she looks out her window or walking down a dusty road with a small child or appearing in a fevered dream that will not be remembered but will only leave the dreamer with the sense of having been visited. She is fierce but gracious; she will not force her way into our midst, but, once invited, will accompany us as tenaciously as a mother bear does her cub.

She will wait outside the city gates as long as it takes, as long as the arguments over her rage, as long as brave souls hazard conversations with her through chinks in the city walls, as long as there are those who risk breathing her name. And when she returns, she will bring with her the others who were outcast, who were lost, who were expelled because of the way they looked or how they acted or what they believed or whom they loved. When she returns, she will bring them dancing into the city, singing in the streets, celebrating in the most sacred places because she has returned, she and those who loved her without even knowing her name all through her long, long exile from home.

# ABOUT THE ARTWORK

*In one of my earliest memories,* I am perhaps five years old. I am standing in my parents' bedroom with a stack of my artwork that my mother has saved. Drawings in pencil and crayon, paintings in tempera and watercolor and finger-paint: this is the artwork that Mom has gathered from my early years. The only stack. And I am systematically tearing up each piece. By the time my mother walks in, I have made it almost to the bottom of the stack. Horrified, Mom asks me why I've done this. "Because they're not any good!" I reply.

I don't know where I got that idea; certainly not at home. My inner critic blossomed early. My heart still hurts for that little girl, her artwork destroyed by her own hand.

Not until two decades later did I seriously begin to pursue visual art. It was the medium of paper collage that enticed me. I had never considered myself particularly adept at drawing, but I found that something magical happened in the process of cutting and tearing and putting the pieces of paper together.

One day, Brother David quizzed me about my fascination with paper. "Where did it come from?" he asked. I remembered the five-year-old girl who had torn up her artwork. I told him the story and commented that perhaps my passion for paper, and for collage in particular, came in part from a desire to put those shredded pieces back together.

I think this is how God works, too. As I piece together the torn and cut papers at my drafting table, the Spirit moves through the scraps and shreds of my own life, fashioning them into something new, something richly textured and colorful and whole.

Most of the artwork in this book is paper collage. A few of the pieces incorporate images that crossed my path, captured my imagination, and challenged my eye: for instance, "Respite in the Land of Red" is composed of images I gathered from other sources. Most of the artwork, however, emerged from my own inquisitive imagination. I used an array of wonderful art papers from around the world, occasionally combining them with other media. Sometimes the final piece resembled what I had initially envisioned; more often, it evolved on the page, taking off in directions I had not anticipated. Such is the mystery of the creative process.

The images that emerge at my drafting table seem to come from a place deeper than words. As a result, I find it much more difficult to gather words to accompany my artwork than to create artwork to go with my words. During the writing of this book, I spent most of my time dwelling in a gap between images and words. The words themselves became a sort of collage as I searched for shreds and scraps of language to articulate what the images stirred within me.

# ACKNOWLEDGMENTS

*Many kind folks helped* create the sacred path that I walked through the seasons of this book. These are some of them.

Sue Joiner, Brenda Lewis, Judy and Joe Richardson, and Skip and Nan Slone witnessed my words, reading the manuscript and providing helpful feedback.

Brother David Liedl, T.O.R., opened wide the door for me to become the artist-in-residence at the San Pedro Spiritual Development Center and helped make a home for me there. The hospitality of the friars, staff, and friends of this Catholic retreat center has helped make it possible for me to live out my vocation as a United Methodist minister.

The congregation of St. Luke's United Methodist Church in Orlando, Florida, provided generous support for my first year of ministry at San Pedro, during which I did the artwork for this book and much of the writing.

Mary Ellen Barrett, Paul Gerardi, Paul Hueber, Maru Ladrón de Guevara, and the Tuesday Group provided wise companionship, deepening my sense of the sacred in the unfolding seasons.

Betsy and Tim Kingsbury, Esther Robinson, and Greta Reed provided hospitality near and far.

Randall Smith did a magnificent job photographing the artwork for the book.

At The Pilgrim Press, Lynne Deming and Kim Sadler welcomed my proposal for *In Wisdom's Path*. Martha Clark, my art director, and Ed Huddleston, the managing editor, tended the manuscript with wisdom and grace. Marjorie Pon and Kathy Method helped guide it through its final stages.

I am grateful.

*For my family*

# INTRODUCTION
## (Or, How This Book Started Out and
## What It Came to Be)

*Like many writers, I write* the introductions to my books last. It seems that only when I have completed the rest of the manuscript can I then look back and have a sense of what it was all about. As I do this, I remember Nancy Mairs's words in the introduction to her book *Ordinary Time,* in which she writes that the only way she can understand her life is "through language, learning line by line as the words compose me. Other people," she goes on to say, "may have developed different and more efficient strategies, but in order to know anything at all, I have to write a book." Now that I'm at the end of this one, I can reflect on what it turned out to be and what I came to know in the course of writing it.

At the outset, I had in mind to write a book that would explore images of and names for God. For quite some time I had lived with the awareness that although one image of God predominates in the Judeo-Christian tradition—that of God as Father—there has always existed a stream, often hidden underground, that runs with other ways of knowing and describing God. That stream flows through the Hebrew and Christian Scriptures, in which writers across the centuries witnessed to God not only with such images as father and king but also with images including mother, midwife, and bakerwoman. The biblical writers also looked to God's non-human creation, describing divinity with such images as eagle, rock, fire, and wind. I believe those writers understood such images of God as metaphors, that they knew that no one image or name or description could contain all of who God is but that each one offered a brushstroke, a glimpse, a point of connection between God and those made in God's own image. As I thought about this book, I envisioned dipping into this stream that flows through the Scriptures and through twenty centuries of Christian tradition, incorporating my own experiences to create a book of reflections, prayers, and artwork that would bear witness to this array of divine images.

I began first with the artwork. This was a switch for me. In my previous book, the artwork had usually followed the writing. I chose with this present book to do most of the artwork first, hoping that without the confines of language, images would surface that might otherwise remain submerged.

And they did. As the artwork emerged, I realized that the images were less about depicting God than about depicting my ongoing search for God. In piecing together the images, I realized I was piecing together a record of a woman struggling to recognize and name and claim the sacred as I experienced it unfolding in my daily life.

The emerging images revealed the change and flux that marked my life in those days. I began this book shortly after moving from my first pastoral appointment, a large United Methodist church in Orlando where I served as the associate pastor for four years. My time at

St. Luke's had been a remarkable experience, a journey of discovery as I became intimately involved in the celebrations and sufferings of this community of folks living within spitting distance of Disney World. It was an experience, too, of intense challenge as I struggled to live out my spirituality and pastoral identity, which were becoming increasingly contemplative, in a three-thousand-member church that was becoming increasingly active. I felt like a "mystic in the megachurch," exhilarated and exhausted by my efforts to create a ministry that would feed and honor both the congregation and myself.

My journey took an unanticipated turn during my fourth year at the church, when the staff-parish committee, after its annual discernment process regarding the pastoral positions, told me they felt it was time for me to "try my wings" and move to a new pastoral appointment, one that they hoped would prove less confining than they thought St. Luke's had been. Although they characterized their decision as being in my best interests, I found myself wondering how their discernment could be for my own good when it had not fully engaged my own self.

And so, in a swirl of emotions, I took wing several months later. With me I carried a deeper sense of myself and of my calling, a keener conviction that I couldn't color inside the lines, and a more intimate knowledge of the ways that brokenness and blessing dwell together.

## GOD IN THE BORDERLANDS

I landed at the San Pedro Spiritual Development Center, a retreat and conference center owned by the Catholic Diocese of Orlando. Situated on four hundred acres of land northeast of the city, San Pedro is run by a small community of Franciscan friars. During my time at St. Luke's I had developed a connection with the center and with Brother David, a friar who directs the San Pedro Center for Art and Contemplation, a ministry which offers opportunities for people to explore the connections between spirituality and the creative process. When it became evident that I would be leaving St. Luke's, David and I began to imagine what it would look like for me to become artist-in-residence at San Pedro. Despite my initial uncertainty about where the financial resources for such a ministry would come from, the necessary doors began to open. St. Luke's opened one of the most crucial doors, with the staff-parish committee and the greater congregation offering funding that would see me through my first year.

Two months after finishing my ministry at St. Luke's, I moved into a small cabin at San Pedro. Nestled in the woods on the shore of a lake, the cabin soon became home as I settled into my new life as artist-in-residence. Sharing in the ministry of the Center for Art and Contemplation, traveling to lead retreats and workshops, spending copious amounts of time at my drafting table or sitting with pen in hand: my life bore a striking resemblance to the dream I had long carried of living out such a ministry.

Moving to San Pedro provided the opportunity to pursue a contemplative and creative way of life with remarkable freedom. As artist-in-residence, I became what the United Methodist Church calls an *extension minister*—a minister who serves "beyond the local United Methodist church in the witness and service of Christ's love and justice" (*The Book of Discipline of the United Methodist Church, 1996*). Such a ministry affords me a unique relationship with the church. I live in some ways on the edges of the institution, and in its borderlands I have staked a claim that allows me to move within several different worlds. This creative space enables me to maintain a deep connection with the church while embracing the freedom to pursue the ministry to which I feel called.

My life in the borderlands has also afforded me a different perspective on God. Leaving congregational ministry, I also left behind many of the protective layers of my life, including significant forms of institutional security and support; a demanding schedule that sometimes insulated me from God, others, and myself; and a work environment in which I was around other people almost constantly. With all that stripped away, a rawness ensued that I found both wondrous and fearsome. In the delicious and staggering solitude of my new life, God challenged me to allow new skin to grow from the rawness, skin that would move more freely, that would be more permeable and transparent, that would allow God and others to see into me, that would allow even me to peer more deeply into myself and perceive the longings and fears and visions that cried out to come forth. In the rawness of the borderlands, God met me and, layer by layer, began to fashion new flesh.

## IMAGINING WISDOM

Although making a home in the borderlands has filled some of my longings, others it has made more keen. For all my solitude, I still carry a deep hunger for community, including a church community. Yet, like many folks, I often feel that when it comes to the church, I am standing in a river, dying of thirst. In worship, I frequently find myself parched by the rituals, the language, the stories that have ignored the voices and experiences of women and others at the margins. But within the stream that runs through our Scriptures and our history, there flow stories, images, and experiences that can heal us. They have been so suppressed and submerged that we will continue to need to scrape our fingers against the bedrock at the stream's bottom in order to reclaim that layer and to free the flow of the current.

In recent years, one divine image that many people have rediscovered is that of Wisdom. In the Hebrew Scriptures and Apocrypha, the Wisdom of God appears as a woman who exists in dynamic relationship with God and embodies attributes of God. In Proverbs and in apocryphal books including Sirach and the Wisdom of Solomon, the writers describe Wisdom (*hokmah* in Hebrew) as a woman who dwelled with God at the beginning of creation, who has an active hand in history, who cries out for justice, who bids us to feast at her table, who calls out to us to follow in her path. In the New Testament, Wisdom does not exist as a woman as such, although references are made to God's wisdom (*sophia* in Greek), and Paul asserts that Christ "became for us *sophia* from God" (1 Corinthians 1:30).

From our perspective in history, we cannot fully fathom the intent of the biblical writers who depicted Wisdom as a woman. They likely drew from a number of influences, including the worship of female deities taking place in the surrounding culture. Whatever her original influences, Wisdom stands as a powerful embodiment of divine activity in the world. One ancient writer describes her this way: "she is a reflection of eternal light, a spotless mirror of the working of God, and an image of God's goodness" (Wisdom 7:26). In depicting Wisdom in this manner, the writers offered an intimate point of connection with God. As with all metaphors, the image suggests but does not encompass the reality. Wisdom not only reveals the divine within herself but also points beyond herself, gesturing toward the rich mystery of the God whom we can never fully capture with any name or image.

In a tradition that emphasizes male images of God to the virtual exclusion of other images, many have found a refuge in Wisdom, drawn to the different face of the divine that she wears. Engaging her, however, calls for discretion, as simply trading a masculine face of God for hers risks missing Wisdom's point. In her book *Praying with Our Eyes Open,* Marjorie Procter-Smith cites Elisabeth Schüssler Fiorenza's conviction that the Sophia tradition "cannot be recovered 'to become the essential feminist tradition of Christianity,' nor does its reconstruction 'necessarily provide a tradition usable for feminists and liberationists.' " Rather, Schüssler Fiorenza understands that our encounter with Wisdom/Sophia can enable us to question, challenge, and change what she calls "ossified and absolutized masculine language" about the divine.

I believe that Wisdom offers a creative call to broaden our understanding of God and of the ways God works in the world. She who danced at creation invites us to move in new ways as God continues to bring the world into being. She offers her own face, her own self, as an image of the divine, but she does not stop there. Wisdom draws us toward the God with whom she dwells, beckoning us into relationship with God. One writer tells us that "in every generation she passes into holy souls and makes them friends of God" (Wisdom 7:27).

Those friends of God who work to unearth different images and names for the divine often do so at risk. In a church that often draws a narrow circle around the divine, those who seek to widen the circle sometimes pose a threat to those invested in the status quo. In our own time, the Re-Imagining Conference, and the wave of outcry against it, stands as one such example. Held in Minnesota in November of 1993, the Re-Imagining Conference took place as part of the World Council of Churches' Ecumenical Decade of Churches in Solidarity with Women. The conference attracted about two thousand participants, most of them women, and brought together a dynamic chorus of voices that offered different ways of reenvisioning God, the church, and the world. For the inclusion of Wisdom/Sophia in the liturgies of the conference, and for other ways they challenged the church, many involved in Re-Imagining encountered accusations of goddess worship, paganism, and heresy, often by those who had little information about what actually happened at the conference. Although addressing the complex issues stirred by the initial conference and by the continuing work of the Re-Imagining Community does not lie within the scope of this introduction, I want to acknowledge one of the many ways the controversy hit home for me.

At the time of the Re-Imagining Conference, which I attended, I was completing the manuscript for a book that for two years had borne the working title *In Wisdom's Path*. As outcry against the conference began to mount, I received a call from my publishing house asking me to drop that title. Fearing that a title using the word "wisdom" would link the book to the Re-Imagining controversy, they requested that I provide a substitute.

After several difficult conversations with the publishing house, I finally agreed. As it turned out, the second choice turned out to be an apt title for that particular work, even as *In Wisdom's Path* became a fitting title for this present book. Although this somewhat mitigated my dismay at changing the title, it did little to assuage my concerns over the widespread backlash against the conference. There were others who paid an infinitely higher price in the controversy, including Mary Ann Lundy, whose departure from her position as the associate director of the General Assembly Council of the Presbyterian Church (U.S.A.) was precipitated by critics of her involvement in the Re-Imagining steering committee.

Offering creative visions of the divine is as necessary as it is risky. Offering those visions does not mean throwing out everything that already exists; rather, I sense the Spirit is challenging us to draw on what we have—to wade into that stream—even as we search for new ways to know God and one another. Exploring the image of Wisdom is one step, but even that will not be enough, for if we stop there, we still limit the dazzling array of ways to describe the divine.

## LANGUAGE AS PILGRIMAGE

Knowing that the naming of God is a journey and not a destination, I seek to describe in these pages the ways I encounter God in some of her forms and in some of his guises. My task is not to replicate the work done by folks who have already offered theological critiques of God-language. Much excellent work already exists which addresses our words about God. What I struggle with here is language *to* God, language which engages me with God, opens me to God, and emerges out of my deepest self. I believe that when it comes to this sort of language, this language to God, we are all pilgrims. The words and images that come in the dark, that take us beyond what we have known, that emerge from the depths of our encounters with one another and with ourselves in all our glory and agony; the words and images that tell honestly of our fears and hopes, our terror and wonder at being living creatures in this world who love and hate and long and ache: this is the language I struggle toward, that I grasp for, that composes me line by line.

As I look back on this book's journey, I remember coming to the realization that, for the most part, I don't have a stash of God-images that I carry around in my pocket. What I do continue to learn is that in encountering different images of God, I grow in my ability to perceive the God who takes flesh in the unfolding moments of my daily life—moments both ordinary and extraordinary. In *Ordinary Time*, Nancy Mairs writes about wanting to examine "this singular absolute of my existence: God is here. And here, and here, and here." In the grit and in the grist. In the struggling and in the resting. In the creating and writing and thinking and praying, in the dailiness of waking and working and eating and loving. God is here, and here, and here, casting a shadow, making a dwelling place, drawing me along the path.

Some time ago, a friend of mine shared with me an African proverb which states, "One hand cannot cover the face of God." It's also true that many hands will never cover the face of God but that when we offer the names and images and visions which come out of our own particular struggles and searching, we widen the circle in which we allow God to dwell. Created in the image of God, we possess a deep connection with the divine. This connection calls us to an endless search during which we may have flashes of insight and recognition and familiarity, yet always an incomplete picture. It is this edge that tantalizes me, calls me, compels me; it is this cusp that draws me into the heart of my life where God dwells and leads me out again.

In these pages, I share my pilgrimage along the edge using the format of the Christian liturgical year. I always seem to return to the rhythms of the liturgical seasons, perhaps because, having spent most of my life in Florida, where the seasons are subtle, I find that following the Christian year is a good way for me to keep time. The seasons of the church offer a rhythm that both stirs up questions and helps me work through them. Within each season, the reflections and prayers offer windows on my struggle to name the sacred as I sense it unfolding in that season.

In the course of the year, Wisdom appears from time to time as a traveling companion, offering both comfort and challenge. According to the ancients, she is intimately acquainted with the seasons, knowing past and future and having "foreknowledge of signs and wonders, of the unfolding of the ages and the times" (Wisdom 8:8, JB). In every time, Wisdom calls us to reach deeply into the stream that flows through the ages, to wade into the waters that sing forth the names of God. There she beckons us to take wisdom and sustenance for the journey that spirals through our lives. In darkness and in daylight, we travel. In season and out. In Wisdom's path.

# ADVENT

## THE CAVE OF THE HEART

*Wisdom is an initiate in the mysteries*
*of God's knowledge, making choice of the*
*works God is to do.*

—Wisdom 8:4 (JB)

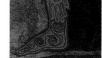

*The image on the slide screen* was cavernous and beckoning. As the gathering in the San Pedro chapel took in the translucent greens and blues of the watercolor, we heard its artist, Sister Doris Klein, C.S.A., offer these words: "In the cave of our hearts . . . in the fabric of our lives . . . in the soul of our earth. . . . you continue, O God, to be born!"

She held the opinion, she said, that Christ was born in a cave. "We all carry a cave," Sister Doris reflected, "a hidden place within us, into which God longs to be born." She told us that Advent is a season to enter that place, to turn inward and encounter the God who seeks to emerge through us.

During the four years that I served as a church pastor, Advent was my busiest season. This past Advent, my first since moving from St. Luke's, was radically different. After a full autumn, my schedule actually slowed down with the onset of Advent. I began to savor the quietness and slowness of the days—taking walks, reading, making notes for a new book, working at my drafting table. But I found myself not feeling terribly Adventish.

Into the midst of this came Sister Doris. As I pondered the image and listened to her words, I realized that in the slowness of the days and the quiet of the season, Advent had been unfolding for me after all.

Shortly after this, I began to reread Meinrad Craighead's book *The Litany of the Great River.* I found myself startled as I came upon a section in which she writes about the cave of the heart. Building her art studio in the Rio Grande valley with a friend one winter, Meinrad thought of the bears that at the same time were gestating their cubs in their mountain caves during the dark season of hibernation. "God lies in the details," she would repeat to herself in her own season of creating. "God lies in the details of all growth and making. I was building my cave, my place to withdraw and hide, the sanctuary where I would birth my images and find God lying in the details."

The ancient writers spoke of Wisdom as an initiate in the mysteries of God's knowledge. I think this is the sort of wisdom we may find in the cave of the heart. When we turn inward, when we give ourselves to the shadows of unknowing, when we open ourselves to God, we are met by One who will be a companion in the mystery and the darkness. This One, too, will help us know what lies for us beyond the cave. That is the other piece of it: the cave of the heart is not a permanent dwelling but a necessary shelter along the way. As an initiate in God's mysteries, Wisdom participates in God's work. We, too, are called: to enter the cave of the heart, to trace the images drawn on its walls, to find God lying in the details of our lives, and then to emerge with newfound wisdom to engage in God's work.

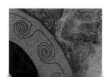

*Begin here. It is raining. . . . I am here alone . . . to take up my "real" life again at last. That is what is strange—that friends, even passionate love, are not my real life unless there is time alone in which to explore and to discover what is happening or has happened.*

—MAY SARTON, *JOURNAL OF A SOLITUDE*

I can hear my pen scratch across the surface of the paper. My windows are open on this Advent evening: rain falls, as it has for much of the day. One lamp in the corner lends a glow to the cabin. I am alone in these woods, writing my way toward my real life. These days, time is measured in books read, in words written, in pieces of colored paper laid across a white page.

Once through the opening, how far is it to the back of the cave of the heart? Tools for measuring the distance don't apply here. Perhaps a new word flung into the darkness periodically to get a sounding, an echo coming back to help me know where I am.

How far? That's not the point. Being here means I've already come a distance. Pondering it is another journey. I begin here.

Thou my source
and my returning,
my beginning
and welcome home,
bless the path
on which I journey;
be the way
that leads me on.

One autumn, while I was still working at the church and had little time for focused writing, I headed up to North Carolina with my laptop computer and my notes for a book I had in the works. I had rented a friend's cabin in the mountains, in an area that is well-populated in warmer months but fairly deserted in colder weather. I arrived as evening approached, shaking off the spookiness as I opened the door and set about to warm up the house. The chill took a long time to dissipate, but the mountain quiet soon settled around me.

For a week I spent the mornings and afternoons intently writing, fleshing out the fragments and lines I had jotted down in a notebook in the margins of my life at home. The rest of the time I spent walking around the lake, reading, and taking time to prepare and enjoy good meals. I spent hours listening to the fabulous public radio station out of Spindale, savoring its folk and bluegrass offerings and encountering singer Gillian Welch for the first time. Each evening I brought up an armload of logs from the basement and built a fire in the fireplace, sometimes sharing it with friends who came to visit.

When I closed the door on that last day, I thought to myself, *This is what I want my life to look like!* Not just for a week or two out of the year, but for good.

My thought became more of a prayer than I anticipated. Less than a year later I became the artist-in-residence at the San Pedro Center, moving into a small cabin there that would become, for a time, my home. Situated on a lake in the woods, the cabin is surrounded by cypress trees and by an astounding array of birds who make the San Pedro property their home. The day I moved in, a pair of sandhill cranes stood in the road at the entrance, as if the official greeters for the long-ago girl who had wanted to become an ornithologist when she grew up.

Here in my cabin in the woods of Florida, I am miles and months away from that place and time in North Carolina. I have found that the daily realities of life impinge upon me more here than they did during my holiday there. This life is no vacation. But I am worlds closer to the rhythm I discovered and longed to take with me as I closed the door on that house in the cold, quiet mountains.

## Building the Fire

Even for this Florida girl,
learning to build a fire
was easy.
It's a matter of preparation:
choose the driest logs
from the basement.
Leave them on the hearth
while you arrange the layers:
first the twigs,
then the shards of wood,
then some crumpled newspaper
on top of that.
How you stack the logs
is a matter of taste;
contact is important,
but they also need room
to breathe.

Touching the match to the kindling,
it's tempting to think
I'm doing this simply
for the heat and light,
that it's not an ancient ritual
borne in my blood,
that it's not a desperate prayer:

*God, set me ablaze.*

Some years ago, my brother through-hiked the Appalachian Trail. Scott and a friend allowed themselves nearly six months to make the 2,159-mile trek from Georgia to Maine. As he prepared for the trip, he would occasionally encounter someone who said, "Man, you're so lucky to be able to take so much time off to do that!" Telling me about one such comment, Scott said, "No luck to it." He'd decided he wanted to do it, and he did what he had to do to make it happen.

Sometimes I have to remind myself that going into the cave of my heart is not a frivolous pastime. It's not a luxury to be worked in as my schedule allows but a necessity for my creative survival, like breathing or eating. Whether it occurs while traveling a trail that stretches for miles or while remaining in one place, making the journey to our center requires more intention than luck. It takes deciding that we'll do whatever is necessary to make it happen.

> The path before me:
> may I walk it in peace.
>
> The path behind me:
> may I leave it in peace.
>
> And the path within me:
> O God,
> may it be peace indeed.

I thought it would never stop raining during the first part of Advent. Day after day the rains came, bringing the lake closer to my door. I had few places I needed to go, so I stayed inside, reading and thinking. As the water drenched the earth, I soaked up words. It was images of God and language about God that I pondered, and I thirstily moved from book to book. Rebecca Chopp, Ada María Isasi-Díaz, Linda Moody and others: a colorful array of women from a variety of cultures offered their names and visions of a God who is intimately involved in the healing and liberation of creation. As the Advent showers continued, the words kept coming. They arrived not so much like rain falling on me, but like water rising, claiming thirsty ground and lapping against a newfound shore.

It wasn't so much that I was looking for different images but for different ways of seeing. I get tired of standing in one place, unmoving. My back starts to ache, my neck grows stiff, my eyes grow tired, the soles of my feet sprout roots that keep me from walking toward others, toward God. Words move me, words and the pondering of them, turning them over in my hands, gazing intently until I see the pattern, the print of the tongue that formed them, the lines and grooves that reveal a whole geography of one who has tasted God, has savored the holy and speaks the words that only she can speak.

God save me
from the people
turning to stone.

God save me
from me
turning to stone.

As the water
wears away the rock,
wash over me.

All that is harmful
bear away
in your flow.

All that would bruise
gather into
your depths.

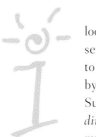 looked into the mirror one day several months after moving to San Pedro and was struck by how tired I looked. Suddenly I thought, *I'm shedding my skin.* I had moved to my new life. I had unpacked my boxes, I had changed my address, I had settled into a different rhythm, but the transformation was still unfolding within me.

I thought about how not all creatures who shed their skins shed them whole. For some, bits and pieces of old skin linger as the new emerges, creating odd patches of dullness against the emerging shiny flesh. That was how I felt, wanting to scrub away all the roughness to emerge fully transformed. But that roughness had protected me in the past, and its flesh was tough. I knew it would take time.

Pondering this, I began to work with images of shedding. I spent a day figuring out how to make a reasonable likeness of snakeskin. (Coating mesh with white printing ink and pressing it on wax paper does the trick.) I found myself curious about why I wanted to stitch the pieces together. In the wild, discarded skin simply crumbles and returns to the earth. Yet I was intrigued by the thought of creating from something so fragile. What are the hands fashioning from the discarded, forgotten flesh? A snakeskin sheet, perhaps, or a sail, or a piece of parchment on which to write the story of how the snake knew, in due season, it was time to let go.

I have a passion for redemption, for taking pieces and fragments and turning them into something new. I've found an artistic hero in my friend Tammy, who proclaims the motto, "Better living through cardboard." With a utility knife and green paint she turned cardboard boxes into an amazing Christmas tree one year, and a four-foot-long angel that she made for me out of a refrigerator box hangs over the archway that divides my cabin. Alice Walker writes "Anything we love can be saved." I'm not sure about that, but I do believe we possess incredible powers of transformation—not of others but of ourselves and the stuff of our lives. Cardboard, memories, stories, choices, flesh, and the human heart: in the creative darkness within us, they can become transformed, reborn, and set free.

Like a rare fruit
peeled back to reveal flesh
startling and sweet,

or an exotic snake
slithering out of her skin
to feel the rough tug of earth
against her belly, vivid and new,

or a flower
that blooms once in a lifetime,
coaxed by the sun
to open petal
by petal,

disrobe me
oh gently,
Companion of my soul.

Shelter my skin
as you trace
its patterns anew.

While doing research for my first book, I became familiar with the work of Julia Esquivel, a Guatemalan poet who spent nearly twenty years living in exile for speaking out against the government. The images in her work, drawn from the decades of oppression that her people suffered in the wake of the CIA-sponsored coup in 1954, continue to haunt and challenge me. In the poem "I Am Not Afraid of Death," from her book *Threatened with Resurrection,* Julia writes of death's "dark and cold corridors" that may yet lead to life. I think that going into the cave of our hearts means that at some point we have to connect with those dark corridors. It means we have to go back far enough into the cave that we begin to hear not only our own inner voice but also the voices beyond us, the voices of people we are called to hear and to be in relationship with. Go far enough, and those voices echo, the voices of the ones whose tongues are scarred from speaking out again and again, the ones in Central America, in South America, in South Africa and elsewhere, the ones who had nearly everything but their voices taken from them. Oscar Romero, Nelson Mandela, Etty Hillesum, the Mothers of the Disappeared . . .

Go far enough into the cave and you will find them, those who know the exact place where contemplation leads to action and reflection gives birth to revolution and prayer gives way to a shattering power that cannot be grasped but can only be received, can only be gathered as the wind is gathered by a sail. Go far enough and you will feel them soaring past you, flying through the dark tunnel toward life, toward birth, hands outstretched in invitation, in liberation, in blessing, in release.

Blessed be the ones
who dance
in the corridors of death,
who sing
in the hallways of terror,
who laugh
in the prisons of fear,
who shout
across the silencing walls,
who love
beyond the borders of hatred,
who live
to welcome home freedom,
who die
never turning their heads,
who return
as the rising of hope.

I have a handful of articles that I have saved over the past few years, pieces that spoke to me and challenged me when I first encountered them and to which I return periodically as my life spirals back around the questions they raised. One of those articles is by former United States poet laureate Rita Dove, an adaptation of an address she gave entitled "To Make a Prairie." She speaks of the absolute necessity of imagination and specifically of the need for daydreaming, a pastime she acknowledges as being increasingly discouraged as we grow up. "There's a loftier expression for it, of course—reverie," Rita writes. "But daydreaming is the word that truly sets us adrift. It melts on the tongue." She quotes French writer Gaston Bachelard, who wrote of a "dreaming consciousness" and called poetic reverie a "phenomenology of the soul" in which "the mind is able to relax, but . . . the soul keeps watch, with no tension, calmed and active."

Rereading the article, I think of how daydreaming affords the opportunity to try on different lives, to make connections that might elude us in more rational moments. It helps account for how a nice Methodist girl like me ended up as the artist-in-residence at a Catholic retreat center. It doesn't make logical sense. But from the time I was a young child, I was given the opportunity to pursue my interests and passions and to see where they led me. I had the time and space for daydreaming and also the support to pursue those dreams. There's still a part of me that never gave that

up. I have spent a lifetime searching my longings, learning and learning again how, if I pay attention to them, they will tell me what I need to know, will give me a map of my heart.

Here,
in the center of my chest,
their constant dwelling:

the persistent yearning
the insistent craving
the unbidden imagining
the desire awakening
the daydream, the nightdream
the reverie unfolding:
the language of longing
drawing me home.

*A great portent appeared in heaven: a woman clothed with the sun,*

*with the moon under her feet, and on her head a crown of*

*twelve stars. She was pregnant and was crying out in birthpangs,*

*in the agony of giving birth.*

—REVELATION 12:1–2

It took three tries to begin to do her justice. In the first rendering, she wore a dress with a golden sun on it and looked very static. I read the story again and realized what it really says: that she was clothed *with the sun,* not with a sunny dress. So the second try had her swathed in the sun itself, with rays etched in gold wrapped around her body.

When I looked at the piece months later, I realized that the gold on the bottom layers of paper had soaked through the upper pieces. It looked unfixable. No matter; I realized I didn't like it so much anyway.

When I returned from a trip to Toronto with some fabulous gold paper from the Japanese paper shop there, I realized it was for her and went, literally, back to the drawing board. As this dark-skinned, dark-haired woman began to emerge, I remembered a poem by Joy Harjo. "Early Morning Woman" tells of a woman stretching in the new day's sun, moving with the strength of the child who grows in her belly. I had used the poem in my first book, in the section about this celestial woman who moves in the agony and hope of birth. Now the early morning woman took shape before me, dazzling in her luminous garb.

I always return to her, to the terror of her birthing and to the force of her loving. In this Advent season, this sun-garbed woman, in labor as a dragon waits to devour her child, reminds me that the cave of the heart is not a place of escape. It is a place to wrestle with those personal dragons that emerge only when we slow down, a place to struggle with those parts of ourselves we hesitate to confront and which we sometimes stifle with too much work or too much play or too many possessions or with substances that dull the ache we cannot name. This struggle is integral to preparing for the labor; it is part of the labor itself. Hiding from myself won't sustain me through the travail, and being merely nice won't give me strength for the birthing, and my silence won't protect what I bring forth from that which seeks to destroy it.

## Sun Woman Speaks

When it was all over
they asked me for a charm
for banishing dragons.

I said
look them in the eye
and call them by name.
It makes them mad as hell,
but they can't abide
the knowing
of their name.

The sun is shining for the first time in a week as I walk to Eucharist this morning. A pale moon, just past full, lingers over the chapel. Later, while doing laundry up the road at the dorm, I stop by the art studio to return a dish to Brother David from a dinner that his class had the night before. He had sent me home with freshly made tabbouleh. He asks me what I am doing today, and I tell him—laundry, reading, a session with my spiritual director this afternoon, and dinner tonight with Amy, who has just returned from spending a year and a half in ministry in South Africa. Perhaps a nap. I tell him of the hibernative state I have been in lately. He reminds me of Sister Doris's words about going into the cave of the heart during this season.

I go back to my cabin and huddle under the covers. I become aware of how my quietness and stillness have to do not simply with weariness but with my body and soul's revolt against the pace I kept for the last four Advent seasons. I haven't done a lick of Christmas shopping, haven't written one card, but today I don't care. I want to lie still and quiet. There are drawings on the walls of the cave of my heart, and with my eyes closed I want to trace each one.

> In the enclosure of your heart,
> O God,
> enfold me
> and give me
> the courage of Bear:
>
> to enter the cave
> in the season of slumber,
>
> to lie down defenseless
> in your gathering dark,
>
> to know your sustaining
> as my soul is made ready,
>
> to give myself over
> to dreaming of birth.

or years I have subscribed to a remarkable magazine called *The Other Side,* a publication which creatively explores the connections between spirituality and social justice. Of the articles I return to periodically, this magazine has supplied most. I have a well-read copy of an article from the July–August 1992 issue, a piece by Dee Dee Risher entitled "A Spirituality of Contentment." As I have worked to sort through what I consider essential in my life, Dee Dee's article has offered wisdom from her own struggle. She writes of days when she felt self-righteous for her chosen self-deprivations, realizing only later that the smugness she felt in simplifying her life masked a deeper discontent. She began to recognize, she writes, that "my external changes had far outpaced my internal transformation."

Dee Dee writes of her struggle with possessions: how their production and ownership affect us and our communities, how they devour our time by the care they require, how they fill up the increasingly larger spaces we sometimes seek so that we have room for all our stuff. Having moved from a four-bedroom parsonage (which I loved) to a one-room cabin (which I also love), I can echo Dee Dee's sentiment that smaller spaces are easier to care for and encourage us to accumulate less.

At the same time, however, Dee Dee asserts that "our spaces must also become places in which our souls feel at home." Acknowledging that they sometimes feel more cluttered than comfortable, she writes, "We should give them some attention—and place in them those things that invite God and others."

I look around my cabin, taking in what I have chosen to place here. My gaze rests on pottery oil lamps and chalices, artwork created both by friends and by people I don't know, and books stacked on every available surface and tucked into every corner. A long, skinny bag from the Blue Moon Bakery in Asheville, North Carolina, which I stuffed with stalks of wheat and mounted on a piece of cardboard that I had painted blue, hangs above the stove. Teacups and mugs descend the wall by the sink on hooks, and tea boxes march along the top of one of the blinds. When one has limited space, dishes and foodstuffs double as decorations.

It is a place of welcome, I think to myself. Here my soul is at home.

O thou who inhabits this dwelling:
Spirit harbored in pots and pans,
dancing in candle and lamp,
lingering in page and pen,
swirling in cup and bowl;

Spirit of wood and wall,
dwelling in threshold and door,
welcoming in table and chair,
delighting in paper and paint;

be revealed in each thing I touch,
be seen in each place I gaze,
be known in each piece I use,
be received in each part of me.

*Advent*

 ome families remember the stories of Advent through keeping the tradition of the Jesse tree, a small tree decorated with ornaments that symbolize the ancestors of Christ. Although this wasn't part of my tradition, somewhere along the way I became aware of the practice. I also learned that the symbols adorning the branches of the Jesse tree tend to represent the male ancestors of Christ more than his female ancestors, probably having to do with the fact that the stories and the lists of begats in the Scriptures tell us much more about the men than the women. The women were there, however, a significant but often hidden stream surfacing occasionally in stories and in places such as the genealogy which opens Matthew's Gospel. Rahab, Tamar, Ruth, Bathsheba, and Mary, the writer reminds us: their blood, too, ran in Jesus' veins.

Thinking of them, I began to imagine another tree, one that grows in a hidden grove, tended by those who know the place. The tree has been nourished by the blood of birthing and by the tears of women who struggled for life. The fires meant to destroy it have thickened its trunk and opened its seeds, which the Spirit has spread to the four corners of the earth. Holding the moon in its arms and the sun in its branches, the tree is witness to the cycles of seasons and the turning of years. I am rooted here, drawing on the strength of generations, listening to the whispered stories in the rustling of leaves. Here all the unremembered, unrecorded names have been traced into the bark. Here the tree grows strong, nourished at the mother root.

Spirit of earth,
take root in me;
strength of fire,
enliven me;
power of wind,
blow through me;
blessing of rain,
fall on me.

Wisdom of blood,
flow through me;
promise of seed,
unfold in me;
endurance of story,
speak through me;
spiral of time,
remember me.

In Florida, a cold snap may come at Christmastime, but it's just as likely that we'll have to run our air conditioners during the holidays. Still, I think something in my blood carries the memories of ancestors who came from colder climes, whose lives were shaped by the turning of the seasons. That's why I was delighted to receive an invitation to a Winter Solstice celebration hosted by Sister Ann Kendrick and the other sisters with whom she shares a home in nearby Apopka. Nearly three decades ago, Sister Ann helped to found the Office for Farmworker Ministries, which works with the large community of people who have struggled to make a living from working on the farms surrounding Lake Apopka. In 1998 the state bought the farms as part of an effort to clean up the lake. In the process, thousands of people lost their jobs and have found little help from the government in making the transition to a new way of life. The sisters continue to engage in creative ministry with the community, bearing powerful witness to the ways the Spirit dwells with the most disenfranchised people.

The Winter Solstice celebration offered a lively, colorful evening of stories and songs shared in Spanish and in English. The sisters' home nearly burst with women connected with the sisters and with the farmworker community. In the company of those women I shared this poem, keenly aware of how they knew in their bones what it means to journey both in darkness and in light.

## A Woman in Winter

A woman in winter
*is* winter:
turning inward,
deepening,
elemental force,
time's reckoning;
sudden frost
and fire's warming,
depth of loss
and edge of storming.

She is avalanche,
quiet hungering,
utter stillness,
snowfall brewing;
hollowed, hallowed,
shadows casting,
field in fallow,
wisdom gathering.

Waiting, watching,
darkness craving,
shedding, touching,
reaching, laboring;
burning, carrying fire
within her,
a woman turning,
becoming winter.

*When Elizabeth heard Mary's greeting, the child leaped in*
*her womb. And Elizabeth was filled with the*
*Holy Spirit and exclaimed with a loud cry, "Blessed are*
*you among women, and blessed is the fruit of your womb. . . . And*
*blessed is she who believed that there would be a fulfillment of*
*what was spoken to her by the Lord."*

—LUKE 1:41–42, 45

For a long time I opened and closed each day with readings from a book called *Earth Prayers,* a lovely and powerful collection of prayers, poems, and invocations edited by Elizabeth Roberts and Elias Amidon. In their introduction to a section of blessings, I found this comment: "Invoking the powers of the universe or bestowing our blessing on the Earth or other beings is neither a simple benevolent wish nor an act of hubris. Rather, it is an act of creative confidence."

I returned to this book as I thought about Elizabeth's blessing of Mary. *An act of creative confidence.* It well describes what takes place between these two women whose pregnancies seem out of season but who navigate God's curious spiral of time with a fierce passion. Elizabeth's blessing of Mary is a full-bodied blessing, springing from the stirring at the core of her being and enfolding Mary, body and soul.

Our English word *bless* comes from the Old English word *blod,* signifying a time when blood was used in acts of consecration. Elizabeth recognizes the sacred blood that she and Mary share, the blood of ancestors running in their veins, the blood they have consented to give to the ones who now inhabit their wombs. Her blessing arises from her blood knowledge, from the wisdom of her womb, and she pours it out to Mary in a powerful act of benediction and consecration.

In blood
be thou blessed.

In flesh
be thou blessed.

In all you choose
in all you hold
in all you gather to you
be thou blessed.

In all you release
in all you return
in all you cast from you
be thou blessed.

In all that takes form in you
be blessed;
in all that comes forth from you
be blessed;
in all thy paths
be thou forever blessed.

In
Wisdom's
Path

*Advent*

# CHRISTMAS DAY

## (December 25)

Among the programs offered by the San Pedro Center is the Audire School for Spiritual Direction Formation, a three-year training program for those interested in becoming spiritual directors. A Latin word meaning "to hear," *audire* is a verb at the heart of the spiritual direction relationship. From September through May we meet once a month, and twice during the year we spend a weekend together. Mysticism was the topic of our instructional weekend last year, focusing particularly on the medieval Spanish mystics St. Teresa of Avila and St. John of the Cross. In the margins of one of our articles from that weekend I scribbled the comment of an instructor who said that John of the Cross maintained we should celebrate Christmas "not only in terms of God coming as a baby but as God marrying the human."

I'm still chewing on what it means for God to wed us, still appalled and fascinated that God would seek us out as partners, as beloved ones, as intimate companions. At mass in the San Pedro chapel one morning, Father Carl spoke of intimacy as a path that leads us into our fears. My spiritual director sounds out *intimacy* as *into-me-see*. Do I want that? Do I want that kind of loving that calls me through my fear instead of around it, that sort of intimacy that beckons me to unhide myself?

## With a Few Lines Borrowed from the Book of Common Prayer

With my body
I thee worship:
with flesh you have fashioned
longing for return,
with heart you have crafted
yearning for repair,
with soul you have tended
aching for communion;

in love and in trepidation,
in doubt and in desire,
for better and for worse,

I take thee
I take thee
I take thee.

*Yet it was you who took me from the womb; you kept me safe on*

*my mother's breast. On you I was cast from my birth,*

*and since my mother bore me you have been my God. Do not be*

*far from me, for trouble is near and there is no one to help.*

—PSALM 22:9–11

Blessed be the ones who help bring forth what is within us.

## The Midwife's Prayer

Keep screaming, little baby girl.
Keep practicing using those lungs
and do not stop,
because hollering will help
to ease the shock
every time you go through
another birth.

Practice squalling
so that your voice is clear and strong
when you speak,
and when your breath
has been knocked from you,
practice breathing small,
but do not stop.

There are miles
of blood vessels in those lungs;
use every inch,
and know the voices
that run in those veins,
the voices that fill your breath,
that will inhabit
your words when you speak
and your groans when you weep
and your mouth when you laugh
and your cries in nights of wild love
and your whispers when you pray.

So keep screaming, little baby girl,
not for that warm, dark place you lost,
but for all the darkness
you will find inside you
that will need to be spoken
with words only you can say.

*Now after the wise men had left, an angel of God appeared to Joseph in a dream and said: "Get up, take the child and his mother, and flee to Egypt, and remain there until I tell you; for Herod is about to search for the child, to destroy him."*

—MATTHEW 2:13

## Departure

Night has fallen again:
the star
gone,
the shepherds
departed,
the angelic voices
stilled,
the wise men
going home
some other way.

The birthing stains on the ground
will soon be covered over
by the traffic of other travelers.

But on the wall of the cave
a bloodied print
the size of the hand of a man
who listened to dreams
and would not leave her,

and the animals
quiet again
but with a knowing look
in their eyes,

and all around
all around
a radiant darkness.

# FEAST OF THE HOLY INNOCENTS
## (December 28)

*When Herod saw that he had been tricked by the wise men, he was*

*infuriated, and he sent and killed all the children in and around*

*Bethlehem who were two years old or under, according to the time*

*that he had learned from the wise men. Then was fulfilled what had*

*been spoken through the prophet Jeremiah: "A voice was heard in*

*Ramah, wailing and loud lamentation, Rachel weeping for her*

*children; she refused to be consoled, because they are no more."*

—MATTHEW 2:16–18

the story of the Holy Innocents reminds me of the shadow side of this season. That the actions of the well-intentioned wise men resulted in such slaughter continues to horrify me. The story stirs up questions about the consequences of my own giving. Particularly in the holiday season, I wonder—who benefits and who loses from the gifts I choose to offer? How much money was earned by the person who actually made the gift? What resources were depleted in its crafting? The questions are complicated and offer no easy answers. I celebrate companies such as Marketplace and Ten Thousand Villages, which offer beautiful work by artisans paid fairly for their labor. I sing gratitude for Alternatives for Simple Living, an organization that offers resources for just and meaningful holiday celebrations. They call us to return to the heart of each holiday, each holy day, bearing gifts that welcome the sacred anew.

Bless the hands
that leave the fingerprints
that tell the story
of every gift:

of those who designed it
and those who crafted;
those who transported it
and those who sold;
those who bought it
and those who profited;
those who gave it
and those who received.

Hallow the circle
of our giving,
hallow the journey
of our gifts,
that in our offering
we may bless
the hands that give
their life to us.

Journeying into and back out of the cave of the heart is a journey of initiation. What gestates within us during seasons of introspection eventually comes to birth and leads us out of the cave, pulling us across a threshold. In my seasons of reflection and introspection, I have learned that I cannot create without being recreated myself. The process changes me, calls forth things from me that I didn't always know were there, leads me to passages and to places I had not anticipated. We who give birth—to children, to dreams, to ideas, to relationships and new ways of living—are ourselves born and reborn as we join in the ongoing cycle of creation.

Many of us live in communities which give little attention to rites of passage, and so we sometimes find ourselves ill equipped to cross the thresholds that appear in our lives: coming of age, leaving home, claiming or changing vocations, entering or leaving relationships, weathering the deaths of loved ones, preparing for our own death, and the myriad other changes in our lives that hold the possibility of rebirth.

In her book *A Circle of Stones*, Judith Duerk asks, "How might your life have been different if there had been a place for you . . . ?" A place to be among women, a place to hear their stories, to receive the generations of wisdom, to honor your body and its cycles, a place where, in time, you would take your place in the circle? Whatever passages we have failed to honor in the past, we can still become intentional about those that lie ahead. Drawing on the wisdom gathered from our introspection, we can emerge from the cave prepared for a new season, a new turn in the spiral.

What we choose
changes us.

Who we love
transforms us.

How we create                    So in all our choosing,
remakes us.                       O God, make us wise;

Where we live                     in all our loving,
reshapes us.                      O Christ, make us bold;

                                  in all our creating,
                                  O Spirit, give us courage;

                                  in all our living
                                  may we become whole.

# EPIPHANY

## SHOWINGS AND ENCOUNTERS

*Wisdom is bright, and does not grow dim.
By those who love her she is readily
seen, and found by those who look for her.
Quick to anticipate those who desire her, she
makes herself known to them. Watch for
her early and you will have no trouble; you
will find her sitting at your gates.*

—Wisdom 6:12—14 (JB)

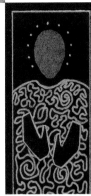

*Epiphaneia: appearance*, manifestation, coming. *Epiphaino:* to give light. *Epephanen:* to be revealed. The Greek words offer a vocabulary for this season, articulating some of the ways that the holy arrives in our midst.

The Feast of the Epiphany began as a festival of the Eastern Church which celebrated the appearing of Jesus, focusing on the events of his birth and baptism. In the Western Christian tradition, Epiphany has traditionally focused on the coming of the wise men to welcome Jesus. At its core this holy day offers an invitation to wrestle with the mystery of the incarnation, to recognize the multitude of ways that the sacred takes flesh, and to welcome the divine into our midst.

The season following Epiphany has become for me a season of thinking about encounters, about the ways that the holy appears in my path, about the wise ones who have journeyed with me for moments or for years and have borne the gifts that I most needed. This season also beckons me to think about the gifts I, too, bear, about the intense responsibility we have to discern what we have to offer and where to offer it.

I experienced this season most keenly during the time in which I knew I would move from my church but could not see the next step on the path. During this season, I had lunch with Bob, a friend and fellow pastor. I told him of my quandary. Knowing of my connection with San Pedro, Bob asked if a ministry there might be possible. I listed the ways that it wouldn't work, and Bob listed the ways that it could, telling me, pointedly, that I needed to pray about it. I wept all the way home, knowing in my heart of hearts that this was what I longed to do. That encounter set in motion a chain of events that propelled me into my position as artist-in-residence at San Pedro, a ministry which has afforded me the opportunity to offer my creative gifts and pursue my passions in a life-giving way.

Wisdom knows the ways we sometimes look far and wide for the knowledge that is right at hand, even already within us. She knows how each moment offers the possibility of an encounter that will draw our eyes from the far horizon toward the God who has already arrived in our midst. From dreams, stories, idle meanderings, and purposeful questions come the messengers who point us toward the sacred guest sitting at the gate of our own soul, seeking the gift only we can offer.

# Feast of the Epiphany

## (January 6)

*In the time of King Herod, after Jesus was born in Bethlehem of Judea, wise men from the East came to Jerusalem, asking, "Where is the child who has been born king of the Jews? For we observed his star at its rising, and have come to pay him homage."*

—Matthew 2:1–2

My friend Carolyn tells a wonderful story of the year when her daughter Jennifer, then a young girl, portrayed a wise man in their church's nativity play. Two of Jennifer's girlfriends also played wise men. Jennifer stirred up a bit of commotion by repeatedly asserting, "We're not wise men, we're wise *women!*" I love the image of this strong girl, now a strong young woman, claiming this name for herself. She, too, has gifts to bear, unique offerings even more precious than frankincense, gold, and myrrh. I long for her defiant words to be on the lips of every girl, for every child, female and male, to gaze at their hands and know that Wisdom's blood runs through them, that the gifts they carry are a treasure, are a blessing, are a grace.

Bless the young one,
the tender one,
the wise child

who comes with hands open,
with eyes wide,
with heart of wonder;

whose blood runs fresh with you,
whose lungs breathe with you,
whose limbs dance with you.

May we see the star that calls her.
May we protect the path he walks.
May we follow where they lead us.

In her novel *The Inhabited Woman*, Gioconda Belli tells the story of the awakening of a woman named Lavinia. Born to a life of privilege in a troubled Latin American country, Lavinia drinks the juice of an orange tree in her yard and becomes inhabited by the spirit of a woman dwelling in that tree. The woman, who centuries earlier had fought against the Spanish conquistadors, settles into Lavinia's awareness, gradually awakening her to the injustices of her own day and stirring her beyond her accustomed complacence toward decisive action.

I believe we carry within us the strength of generations and that we, too, are inhabited by those who have gone before: by their brokenness and the pain that their decisions have sometimes inflicted upon us, yes, but also by their wisdom, by the courage of their choices made for healing and freedom. There are wise ones who inhabit our blood, their dreams and hopes flowing through us, their voices echoing in the pounding of our hearts.

God of the generations,
when we set our hands to labor,
thinking that we work alone,
remind us that we carry
on our lips
the words of prophets,
in our veins
the blood of martyrs,
in our eyes
the mystics' visions,
in our hands
the strength of thousands.

ne of my favorite singer-musicians is Loreena McKennitt. With melodies and lyrics drawn from ancient sources and from her travels around the world, Loreena's songs haunt me. Even her original works possess an old spirit, imbued with Loreena's fascination with the sacred sites and stories of diverse peoples. Her liner notes alone are worth the price of her compact discs; she writes movingly of the travels and reading that formed the strains of each song.

In the notes to her compact disc *The Visit,* Loreena writes of the creative impulse as "a visit—a thing of grace, not commanded or owned so much as awaited, prepared for." It is also a mystery, she observes, whose arrival prompts us to ask, "Who is this, and what is here?" as King Arthur's knights do when they lay eyes upon the enigmatic Lady of Shallot.

*Who is this, and what is here?* I carry these questions throughout this season, asking them of myself, of God, of those whom I encounter, and of what takes form beneath my creating fingertips.

## Breathing the Water

All that I was born remembering
began to escape with my first cry.
It was not the cold
that I wailed against,
or the insulting light,
but the threat of forgetting
everything I had known.

This poem is a prayer,
a dreaming toward the place
where I knew how life happened:
the dividing of cells,
the forming of flesh,
the branching of veins,
the sculpting of bones.

This creating is a remembering,
a walking toward
the midnight muse
who recalls how to breathe
the water,
who waits at the bottom
of my dark stairs,
bidding me descend.

n top of the cabinet above my kitchen sink sit a chalice and plate. Fired in earthy shades of green, they serve as reminders of the sort of encounter I experience from time to time and which I treasure, when someone crosses my path for perhaps the only time, passing along a gift I will always carry.

While on vacation several years ago in Maine with my sister and her family, I browsed through a jewelry shop with Sally one after-noon. I spotted a beautifully designed pendant made of deep, fiery opals. The women in my family have a genetic weakness for opals, and I fell in love with this piece on first sight. I don't wear much jewelry, but it took little encouragement from my sister to purchase this piece. The woman who crafted the pendant also owned the store and was there that day. We ended up visiting for a time. She shared a loaf of wondrous Italian bread with us and told us of her home in Tuscany, where she lived part of the year. She taught us a phrase she learned there: *speriamo*. "It means 'we can always hope,'" she told us.

Upon learning that I lived in Florida, the jeweler pulled out her business card and turned it over. "I used to live there on a houseboat," she said as she began to draw a map on the card. "I worked with this potter on Merritt Island. He still has a shop there—you should go check it out." Some time later, I did. In the shop connected to his studio, tucked among the trees, I found this chalice and plate, fired in shades of earth, of ocean water, of the opals I wore. I have celebrated Communion with the set many times, and when I pass the loaf and share the cup, I remember the jeweler's bread that she offered with a blessing: *speriamo*. We can always hope.

That peace
will rise like bread
we can always hope.

That justice
will flow like wine
we can always hope.

That the table
will make strangers kin
we can always hope.

That our hope
will rise like bread
we can always pray.

Preparing to leave St. Luke's and set off for worlds barely known proved to be a tumultuous journey. Excited about what lay ahead, I also struggled with the grief involved in getting there. At the time I felt I had to keep a tight rein on my emotions so that I could get through the leave-taking with grace. After I moved, I found it difficult to reconnect with my long-stifled emotions. I knew they lay seething under the surface and that my difficulty in acknowledging them was contributing to my ongoing weariness.

During this time I had several dreams in which I gave myself over to the grief and anguish which I resisted in my waking life. Usually there was someone with me, a companion who not only witnessed but also helped to call forth the torrent of emotion that I had studiously kept in check. Sometimes I knew the person from my waking life, sometimes not. Yet in the presence of the visitor I felt safe enough to release the flood. The dreams became a doorway into my waking life. Walking across their threshold, I began to reconnect with what lay churning under the surface of my life and to move toward newfound energy and healing.

God of the torrents,
not for containment
of this blessed rage
but for this I ask:
strength to burst
the vessel
that keeps it bound
and for grace
to take the pieces
and form
not a fence
around its danger
but a path
through its power.

A long time ago I became fascinated by the tradition of the giveaway practiced among many Native American nations. Typically taking place in ceremonial gatherings, the giveaway affords the opportunity for the community to honor certain members. In return, the honorees offer gifts to others to whom they want to show their appreciation and gratitude. I have heard it said that in societies which practice the giveaway, wealth is measured not by what one possesses but by what one gives away.

I have heard, too, that gifts offered in the giveaway sometimes include possessions that the giver has long treasured. This generosity in particular beckons me to ponder my own practices of giving. I believe that objects soak up some of the spirit of their owners, and that when we give someone a possession that has meant a great deal to us, we pass on part of our own essence. Books are among my most valued belongings, and I love to give away volumes that I have found significant in my journey. Yet as I write this, I'm aware that it has been quite some time since I have let any of my treasured books go. I believe there needs to be a certain amount of flow to our belongings and that those of us who have plenty of material things would do well not only to rid ourselves of some of what we don't really need but also to give away some of the possessions most dear to us. I find this a huge challenge. Scanning my own small space, I wonder, *could I give this away? Could I let go of that?*

That our receiving
may be like breathing:
taking in,
letting go.

That our holding
may be like loving:
taking care,
setting free.

That our giving
may be like leaving:
singing thanks,
moving on.

during the months in which I knew I would be moving from St. Luke's but did not yet know where I would go, I facilitated a class at the church based on the book *The Artist's Way* by Julia Cameron. I had picked up the book a year or so earlier, thinking it looked intriguing, and then set it aside. When I returned to it, I realized that, because of the work Julia asks the reader to do in the course of the book, it would be helpful to go through it with a group that would hold me accountable. I offered a class at the church, thinking that if we had at least eight people, the class would be a go.

We had more than twenty people in the class. Spanning six decades in age and a wide variety of backgrounds, we had each come with a desire to stretch ourselves and a longing to explore the ways that the creative spirit moved through our lives. The course provided both a haven of comfort and a swift kick in the rear for me. Throughout the book, Julia prompts the reader to pay attention to the dreams and longings dwelling inside us, dreams which may have been squelched, suppressed, denied, ridiculed, forgotten, or simply left to languish. Those dreams serve as a map, she believes, and can lead us to a place where we must choose to make a leap of faith or turn away once again.

When the door to becoming artist-in-residence at San Pedro began to open, significant obstacles remained, including the fact that San Pedro had no money for such a position. I knew that this was what I longed to do, and Julia's words served as balm and goad as I took the leap and a way began to emerge. In the draining and exhilarating time of planning and transition, she reminded me of the gamut of emotions often present when seeking to claim and offer one's gifts. "A certain giddiness may accompany sudden stabs of loss," she writes. "Think of yourself as an accident victim walking away from the crash: your old life has crashed and burned; your new life isn't apparent yet. You may feel yourself to be temporarily without a vehicle. Just keep walking."

JUST KEEP WALKING.

Made from earth I am
and in love with the ground,
but this urging persists,
an aching where you etched
onto tendon muscle bone nerve
a longing for leaping,
a yearning to soar.

# BAPTISM OF JESUS

## (First Sunday after Epiphany)

Then Jesus came from Galilee to John at the Jordan, to be baptized by him. John would have prevented him, saying, "I need to be baptized by you, and do you come to me?" But Jesus answered him, "Let it be so for now; for it is proper for us in this way to fulfill all righteousness." Then he consented. And when Jesus had been baptized, just as he came up from the water, suddenly the heavens were opened to him and he saw the spirit of God descending like a dove and alighting on him. And a voice from heaven said, "This is my Son, the Beloved, with whom I am well pleased."

—MATTHEW 3:13–17

## Jordan

More than once today
I have thrown down
my notebook,
my pen,
and finally myself
onto this bed.

Jordan springs from either eye,
and it may look
like I am weeping
from this wrestling,
but really I am
standing at the water,
looking for the one
who will pull me under
and holler out my name.

he shedding process of leaving the church and settling in at San Pedro left me feeling utterly raw during my first few months as artist-in-residence. Raw from leaving behind the familiar, raw from leaving a certain amount of security, raw from moving more deeply into a creative life. I reveled in spending long hours at my drafting table, where before I fit my art into my schedule as I was able. But as the images came, I felt exposed.

I remembered going to the dedication service for the San Pedro Center for Art and Contemplation the year before. The dedication coincided with the Feast of the Stigmata of St. Francis, a Franciscan celebration which commemorates Francis's receiving the wounds of Christ. In his comments at the dedication, Brother David shared some of St. Bonaventure's reflections on Francis's stigmata. Bonaventure, himself a Franciscan, wrote that when Francis received Christ's physical wounds, it was a manifestation of a transformation that had already taken place within himself. Francis had already conformed himself to the love and passion of Christ, Bonaventure wrote. The stigmata made visible what was already present within Francis.

"Francis was an artist," David went on to reflect. "But more important, he was a lover: he had a passion for life, a passion for people, and a passion for God. This beloved man of all peoples revealed his deepest passion, visible now in his very flesh." The artist, David observed, is called to reveal such passion. "Artists risk the vulnerable stance when they open themselves to life. The artist, the crafter of life, gathers in through the senses all of life, the good, the bad, the grit and the grime, the pleasure and the pain, the memories and the dreams. And, in embracing everything, the artist shatters the limits of reason,

purpose, and duty to risk showing the world what is inside their heart and our hearts."

David, again: "Some artists present to us their own woundedness. Some artists show us the woundedness of the world. But all artists, like Francis, show us the great wound, the wound of the heart. It is the great wound of the heart transformed, transubstantiated, if you will, into beauty because what they present to us is the image of Love."

As I fingered my wounds during those months, I contemplated David's words. They didn't ease my feeling of exposure, but they did help me to give it a name. I am still coming to understand my wounds as a doorway, one through which I risk showing my inner world to others and one through which I walk toward healing.

Carve it into my flesh
if you must, Creator God;
Artist God, Passionate God,
inscribe it into my palms
so that I do not forget
what you made me for.

But do not forget to tend me,
to touch the wounds exposed,
to hold the raw and aching heart
that pulses with your
fierce and piercing art.

In
Wisdom's
Path


*Epiphany*

Looking through catalogs and magazines in a search for images and inspiration, I became fascinated by a series of masks that I found. As I drew and pieced together this picture, I thought it was about the different faces that God wears. As I continued to work on it, I began to think, *the masks are our own.* Perhaps the truth is that we are on a journey both to recognize God in all her guises and also to learn how to show our true faces to God and one another.

I can barely ask you
to unmask me
for fear your touch
on my face
would shatter skin.

And yet,
shed of every guise,
I long to be
in your gaze
beheld,
in your sight
beloved,
in your presence
bereft
of all that keeps me
unrevealed.

On the third day there was a wedding in Cana of Galilee, and the mother of Jesus was there. Jesus and his disciples had also been invited to the wedding. When the wine gave out, the mother of Jesus said to him, "They have no wine." And Jesus said to her, "Woman, what concern is that to you and to me? My hour has not yet come." His mother said to the servants, "Do whatever he tells you." Now standing there were six stone water jars for the Jewish rites of purification, each holding twenty or thirty gallons. Jesus said to them, "Fill the jars with water." And they filled them up to the brim. He said to them, "Now draw some out, and take it to the chief steward." So they took it. When the steward tasted the water that had become wine, and did not know where it came from (though the servants who had drawn the water knew), the steward called the bridegroom and said to him, "Everyone serves the good wine first, and then the inferior wine after the guests have become drunk. But you have kept the good wine until now." Jesus did this, the first of his signs, in Cana of Galilee, and revealed his glory; and his disciples believed in him.

—John 2:1–11

Jesus knew that from the ordinary, the extraordinary comes. To heal a blind man, he used dirt and spit; to feed the multitudes, he used common bread and fish; to speak of God, he used yeast and seeds. He knew the truth of how the mundane gives way to the miraculous: fill enough jars with water, one of them might turn to wine.

## And You Said

Where there was no wine
there was you
and you said drink,
and there it was,
startling and sweet.

And where there was no bread
there was you
and you said feed one another,
and there it was,
filling and strong.

And where there was no love
there was you
and you said touch,
and there we were,
our hands looking like yours.

When I first saw this figure, its arms outstretched, I thought of resurrection, of Christ emerging from the tomb. As I worked with it, the awareness began to settle in that the shape is not a silhouette but a shadow. I remembered learning as a child how sometimes we can see things more clearly with our peripheral vision than by looking straight on, how stars, for instance, may reveal themselves to the corner of one's eye more easily than to the center. Sometimes we can come to know a thing only by averting our gaze, by not shocking it with the full force of our looking. Some things, too, long to be known first in shadow. I think that God is sometimes like this: teasing, dancing on the edges of our awareness. I think God does this not because God is mean or coy but because God longs to be courted, to dwell in a mystery that keeps us aching to touch the skin beneath the shadow.

I have sought you
in daylight
as if the discovery of you
would not scorch my eyes,
singe their lashes,
sear their brows;
as if your gaze
would not unface me,
lay bare every longing,
devastate all my knowing.

And here you are,
teasing the corner of my eye,
offering peripheral visions,
knowing
that what can't be borne
in sunlight
may still be known
in shadow.

In

Wisdom's

Path

*Epiphany*

The night before I left Atlanta, where I went to seminary, to move back to Florida, I gathered with friends at Lori's apartment. Candles flickered in the shadows as we talked into the night. Before I left, Lori gave me two purple candles to take with me. Especially during that first year back in Florida, I lit them when I longed for a sense of connection with people who knew me well. Though I tried to use them sparingly, after a time they had burned down to nubs.

I wrote to Lori and told her what the candles had meant to me, told her of the light they had provided in a time of shadows. I said that certainly I could go buy more candles but that I was trying to learn how to ask for help when I needed it. Could she send me another candle?

One gray day during a difficult season, a package from Lori appeared in my mailbox. I opened it and caught my breath as I pulled out a beautiful pottery oil lamp. I filled it with oil, struck a match to its wick, and let it burn most of the day, blowing it out only to rest. The gift of light was a gift of grace. It did not take the shadows away, but it did remind me of those who were present with me in my questions and in my sorrow.

God of the shadows,
you know
how I have loved the darkness,
its enticing mystery,
its intimate depths.

And also you know
how I have longed for the light,
for the spark in the shadows
that brings vision and warmth.

Hold me together
in all of my turnings
from shadow to sunlight,
from full day to night.

Bless me for loving
the quickening edge
and the hope that it offers
for glimpsing your face.

*And having been warned in a dream not to*

*return to Herod, the wise men left for their own*

*country by another road.*

—MATTHEW 2:12

It's been another day of detours. I am not where I thought I would be but am amazed by the stars I am finding in my skies lately. In the liner notes to her compact disc *The Book of Secrets,* Loreena McKennitt writes, "In the end, I wonder if one of the most important steps on our journey is the one in which we throw away the map. In jettisoning the grids and brambles of our own preconceptions, perhaps we are better able to find the real secrets of each place."

God beyond borders,
may I wander
with wanting enough
to unlearn my path,
with wonder enough
to receive the secrets of each place,
with wisdom enough
to allow them to whisper me
home a different way.

# FEAST OF ST. BRIGID
## (*February 1*)

 ne of my favorite saints is St. Brigid (also spelled Brigit, Bridget, or Bride), a Celtic woman who lived from 454 to 524 C.E. Born to one of her father's slaves, a woman named Broicsech, Brigid grew up in the home of a Druid who became her mentor and friend. Brigid eventually became a nun and went on to found a renowned monastery for women and men in the town of Kildare.

Fascinating legends surround Brigid, partly because there was a pre-Christian Celtic goddess of the same name, spelled Brigit or Brighid. A goddess of wisdom, poetry, and song, Brigit was also the goddess of healing and of metalworking. Traits and legends of the goddess Brigit seem to have been woven into the story of the historical Brigid, producing rich tales of a woman known for her compassion, wisdom, and miracle-working.

The goddess Brigit was also the goddess of fire and the hearth, and legends about St. Brigid associate her closely with fire. One story tells of a pillar of flame that stretched from her head to the heavens when she was born, and another story tells of a similar flame which appeared at the moment Brigid took her monastic vows.

Many legends refer to St. Brigid as the midwife to Mary during Jesus' birth and as his foster mother, a role the Celts considered at least as important as that of the biological mother. One of my favorite legends describes Brigid's quick thinking in the face of danger. As Mary, Jesus, and Joseph flee Bethlehem for Egypt, Brigid spots King Herod's soldiers entering the town. Brigid quickly makes a crown of candles and dances in front of the soldiers,

distracting them as the holy family escapes to safety.

According to legend, Brigid's mother gave birth to her while crossing the threshold into the house, one foot outside the doorway and one foot inside. Brigid remains on the threshold as a bridge figure between pre-Christian and Christian spiritual traditions. I think she has many secrets and much to tell us. I think she holds a deep well of wisdom for those who seek to honor the past as we discover the sacred in the present.

## St. Brigid's Round

In the burning fire,
in the dancing flame,
she gives her heart,
and she takes her name;

she will not be tamed,
she will never tire
of the dancing flame
of the burning fire.

In the dancing flame,
in the burning fire,
she will not retreat,
she will not retire

from the insight clear,
from the blessings claimed
in the burning fire
in the dancing flame.

# CANDLEMAS

## (February 2)

forty days after Jesus' birth, Mary and Joseph went to the Temple for the presentation of Jesus and the purification of Mary, as was the Jewish custom following a birth. Luke's Gospel tells of their welcome by the prophet Anna and by Simeon, both of whom had long awaited this child. Upon seeing Jesus, Simeon takes him into his arms and speaks of him as "a light for revelation to the Gentiles." Because of Simeon's words about light, this day—called the Feast of the Presentation or the Feast of the Purification of Mary—became in many places a day to bless the candles that would be used in the coming year. In England, this candlelight service became known as "the Candle Mass," giving rise to the name Candlemas.

In his notes to *Carmina Gadelica*, a remarkable collection of Celtic blessings, prayers, hymns, and incantations, Alexander Carmichael writes, "It is said in Ireland that Bride [St. Brigid] walked before Mary with a lighted candle in each hand when she went up to the Temple for purification. The winds were strong on the Temple heights, and the tapers were unprotected, yet they did not flicker nor fail." Carmichael observes that because of this, Brigid is called *Bride boillsge* (Bride of brightness) and that some call this day *La Fheill Bride nan Coinnle* (the Feast Day of Bride of the Candles) or, more commonly, *La Fheill Moire nan Coinnle*—the Feast Day of Mary of the Candles.

Bless those
who know the darkness
and do not fear it,

who carry the light
and are not consumed,

who prepare the way
and will not abandon it,

who bless with grace
that does not leave us.

A recurring dream began to visit me a couple of years ago. Some of the details change, but the essence remains the same: I am wandering through shops—not a mall, but a series of connected stores. They are stores of the sort I love to browse through, the kind I find in communities which value artistry. I savor what I see as I wander through the stores: richly hued artwork, finely crafted jewelry, beautiful pottery which calls out for me to touch and hold it.

I always find a bookstore in the dream. One time it was a used bookstore, crammed with volumes and with more shelves around every turn. Another time it contained a case of gorgeous hand-bound books, displayed like artwork. I marveled at the colors, textures, and designs, knowing as I touched the books, *I want to do this, to create volumes like these.*

One of the things that intrigues me about the recurring dream is that it almost always begins with my walking down a familiar street. I turn a corner and suddenly find myself at the shops, thinking to myself, *Of course—THAT'S where they were!* They lay in my neighborhood the whole time, waiting to be found.

WAITING TO BE FOUND.

# touch the
## DEPTHS

Giver of the dream,
this I ask:

for courage
to take the paths
the feet of my soul
have always known;

for vision
to see the wonders
the eyes of my longing
would never forget;

for stillness
to hear the song
the ear of my spirit
will ever remember;

for daring
to taste the delights
the tongue of my heart
forever recalls;

for wisdom
to touch the depths
the hands of my desire
could never erase.

In
Wisdom's
Path

*Epiphany*

# SHROVE TUESDAY

A moveable feast, Shrove Tuesday falls the day before Ash Wednesday. Its name derives from the custom of being shriven (confessing and being granted absolution by a priest) in preparation for the season of Lent. It is also called Fat Tuesday (*Mardi Gras* in French) from the old Roman Catholic practice of using up all the remaining fat in one's kitchen prior to entering a season of fasting.

For some years, I found Lent a tremendously difficult and draining season. As each Lenten season rolled around, I had occasion to deal with a death or some other painful ending. One year, as spring approached, I began to experience an inexplicable sense of dread. Then it hit me: Lent lurked just around the corner. My soul, unbeknownst to me, had already started to gear up for the season.

That year I decided to have a Shrove Tuesday celebration. On the eve of Lent, I wanted both to celebrate significant healing that had taken place in my life and to set the tone for what I hoped would prove a less draining season. I invited a group of friends to my home, asking each to bring a dish for the meal, a candle, and some words that spoke of healing and change.

We had a festive evening as we gathered around the table for the Fat Tuesday feast and as we shared words that prepared a path for the season ahead. As we ended the evening, we gathered in my foyer. A circle of women stood on the threshold with lighted candles in their hands, offering words of blessing for the journey past and the journey ahead. They left their candles in the foyer when they departed, and I remained there for a while, watching the flames of their leftover lights. The women's voices echoed on the threshold, and I wrapped their words around myself and waited for the coming season.

Many hands for the turning,
many flames for the burning,
many words for the learning,
I gather them all.

In my spiraled returning,
in my unceasing yearning,
may the ones who enfold me
deliver me home.

DELIVER ME HOME.

# LENT

## ART FROM THE DARK

*Yahweh created me [Wisdom] when God's purpose first unfolded, before the oldest of God's works. From everlasting I was firmly set, from the beginning, before earth came into being. . . . I was by God's side, a master crafter, delighting God day by day, ever at play in God's presence, at play everywhere in the world.*

—Proverbs 8:22—23, 31—31a (JB)

$\mathcal{B}rowsing$ $through$ $the$ San Pedro bookstore one day, I came upon *The Psalter*, a translation of the psalms crafted by the International Commission on English in the Liturgy. I found myself enchanted by the artwork which accompanied the psalms. Black-and-white monotype prints, created by artist Linda Ekstrom, graced the pages. They conveyed the starkness and the shadows of the psalms and offered what Ekstrom calls respite in the vast sweep of the psalms, a place for the eye and soul to rest.

I was fascinated. I wanted to learn how to do this. My instruction in monotype printmaking came from Linda's notes on the artwork, in which she writes, "Black etching ink is wiped from a plate with brush, cloth and palette knife to create or to 'find' an image. In the transformation from ink plate to paper there is an element of surprise where mystery appropriately enters." I gathered the tools and went to work.

The seeming simplicity of Linda's images proved deceptive. As I began to experiment with the technique, I became increasingly confounded. I wanted my prints to look like Linda Ekstrom's. Each time I pulled the paper from the inked glass, what I got was, well, *me*.

When I stopped picking up the psalter with my ink-laden hands, looking at Linda's illustrations and thinking, *How did she do that?*, I started exploring the images that the glass and ink beckoned from my own soul. Monotype printmaking was a radical shift from paper collage, my primary medium and my first artistic love. Where collage art involves creating by piecing together and building up the surface, monotype printmaking requires erasure and wiping away. It's the difference between addition and subtraction. Learning to make monotype prints meant learning to start from the dark.

It's where we start in the season of Lent, too. The season begins with ashes and invites us into a time of stripping away all that distracts us from recognizing the God who dwells at our core. Reminding us that we are ashes and dust, God beckons us during Lent to consider what is elemental and essential in our lives. As a season of preparation for the mysteries of death and resurrection, it is a stark season. Yet, as in Linda Ekstrom's haunting images, a raw beauty permeates these days. In fire, wind, earth, and water—elements that permeate the words and images of this section—we find the building blocks for creating anew.

In Proverbs, Wisdom sings of her role in creation, of her presence as God began with the darkness and fashioned the world. She offers delight as she beckons us, too, to create, to take what we find in the shadows of our lives and craft what never before has been seen.

*And the Spirit immediately drove Jesus out into the*
*wilderness. He was in the wilderness forty days,*
*tempted by Satan; and he was with the wild beasts;*
*and the angels waited on him.*

—MARK 1:12–13

I intended for the space in the center of this piece to be solid black. but there was grit in the ink. When I pulled the paper from the inked glass. stars emerged. I thought of Jesus in the wilderness. for forty days and nights coming face-to-face with the essence of who he was. In other Gospel accounts of this story. the writers include the questions posed to Jesus by Satan. Intended to entice and distract him. the questions have the converse effect of helping to clarify what lies at Jesus' core.

Humans do not live by bread alone. Jesus said in that wilderness. But I imagine angel-borne bread at the end of those forty days. coming to ease his hunger. to sustain him for the path ahead.

I am not asking you
to take this wilderness from me,
to remove this place of starkness
where I come to know
the wildness within me,
where I learn to call the names
of the ravenous beasts
that pace inside me,
to finger the brambles
that snake through my veins,
to taste the thirst
that tugs at my tongue.

But send me
tough angels,
sweet wine,
strong bread:
just enough.

ver the years I have become fascinated by the reemergence of the labyrinth as a tool for contemplation. Distinct from a maze, in which one often encounters many dead ends before reaching the center, a labyrinth is unicursal: the one path in is the one path out. The labyrinth dates back thousands of years, with different forms of it having emerged in disparate cultures.

On the floor of Chartres Cathedral in France lies a large labyrinth which was worked into the stone during construction of the cathedral in the thirteenth century. During the Middle Ages, many Christians who could not make a pilgrimage to the Holy Land walked the labyrinth. This walking became a form of pilgrimage; as the seeker trod the path, the twists and turns offered the opportunity to make a sacred journey within.

I first walked a labyrinth during a Lenten retreat at the San Pedro chapel. Painted onto a large canvas, this replica of the Chartres labyrinth nearly filled the chapel. My most moving moment came not while I walked the labyrinth but as I sat resting on the floor, watching other participants slowly walk the path. I was in the midst of preparing to leave St. Luke's and move to San Pedro, and I found myself struck by the vivid tableau before me. It captured the essence of what I had hungered for, and what I had begun to claim: a space to move slowly, to walk the path at my own pace.

## Walking Blessing

That each step
may be a shedding.
That you will let yourself
become lost.
That when it looks
like you're going backwards,
you may be making progress.
That progress is not the goal anyway,
but presence
to the feel of the path on your skin,
to the way it reshapes you
in each place it makes contact,
to the way you cannot see it
until the moment you have stepped out.

everal years ago I traveled to Arizona at the invitation of a friend. Winging my way westward, I watched in awe from the airplane window as the landscape began to change. I had worn my hiking boots on the plane, and my host took me immediately from the airport into the Tucson desert for a hike. I felt as though I had been dropped onto another planet, yet I had hungered for years to see this earth.

I thought of Joan Sauro's book *Whole Earth Meditation,* her powerful reflection on what she calls "an ecology for the spirit." "Go to the place called barren," she writes. "Stand in the place called empty. And you will find God there. . . . God always breaks through at your weakest point, where you least resist. God's love grows, fullness upon fullness, where you crumble enough to give what is most dear. Your earth."

## Warning
### for P.G.

Before you enter this terrain
there are a few things
you should know.

There is no entry fee,
but it will cost you plenty
to make this journey.

Pack a lunch. Lose your map.
Travel lightly. The weather
is unpredictable.

I am prone to sudden washouts,
to the startling crumbling of earth.
It's good to watch your step,
but what is underneath is strong
and you are welcome to settle there
to rest for the night
or to stay for a season.

Be careful at dusk.
It's when the beasts come to the water,
and it's not that they would devour you,
but they are protective of their terrain
and will not easily yield.
I can tell you
they will never be utterly tamed,
but with choice morsels
and soothing words,
you may have them
eating from your hands.

If these warnings sound harsh, good;
this terrain is not
for the faint of heart
or for those who would travel
its contours crudely,
littering its landscape
and stripping its soil.

But I think you are made
of stronger stuff
and more tender,
that you already know
the lay of this land:
how its treasures will yield
to your searching fingers,
how its wellsprings will ease
your traveler's thirst,
how its brambles and thorns
will give way
to the waiting hidden garden
where grows the sweetest,
most exquisite fruit
waiting to be consumed.

"to the place called barren."

In monastic communities around the world, the hours are kept sacred. The ebb and flow of darkness is marked by the daily offices, the times when the community gathers to pray, to contemplate Scripture, to chant the psalms. Matins, lauds, prime, terce, sext, none, vespers, compline: although some communities abbreviate the schedule, these prayer offices make up the ancient rhythm of prayer known as the Liturgy of the Hours. In *The Cloister Walk,* Kathleen Norris observes that liturgical time "is essentially poetic time, oriented toward process rather than productivity, willing to wait attentively in stillness rather than always pushing to 'get the job done.' "

During my stay in Tucson I spent a night at the house of the Benedictine Sisters of Perpetual Adoration. I joined the sisters for their night prayer and then talked over tea with the newly chosen abbess far into the night. After getting ready for bed, I walked through the door that connected the guest quarters to a small balcony overlooking the chapel. Candles still burned, and the fragrance of incense lingered in the air. I sat in the balcony, keenly aware of the prayers spiraling around the chapel, enfolding me in their rhythm of night into day into night.

God of the ages,
to whom the hours
are nothing
and everything:

may I know each moment
as a sacred guest
to be welcomed,
to be savored,
to be sent
with a blessing.

**B**rowsing through a bookstore during Lent this year, I came across Carol Lee Flinders's book *At the Root of This Longing.* I took it home and devoured it in a few days, intrigued by her effort to reconcile what she called "a spiritual hunger and a feminist thirst." Early in the book she writes about a piece of synchronicity that returned her to the work of Julian of Norwich, an English mystic who lived during the fourteenth and early fifteenth centuries. Julian lived as an anchoress, never leaving the tiny cell attached to the Church of St. Julian in Conisford at Norwich, where she dwelled with her cat and visited with folks who came to her window seeking counsel. At the age of thirty and a half, Julian received a series of visions which she recorded in a short text. After reflecting on the visions for about twenty years, Julian set them down in a longer text. Together these texts became known as *Revelations of Divine Love,* or, more commonly, *Showings.*

Reading Carol's book reawakened my own interest in Julian. Some years before, I had read *Showings* as part of my research for *Sacred Journeys.* At that time, I had read it at a brisk pace, seeking to absorb what little is known about Julian and to gather quotations of her work to include in my book. As Lent progressed this year, I returned to Julian's remarkable work, this time reading more slowly. In the mornings I would light a candle and open to her words. "All will be well," she reminded me, "and every kind of thing will be well." "We can never come to the full knowledge of God," she told me, "until we first clearly know our own soul." And this, too, she said: "As truly as God is our Father, so truly is God our Mother."

Carol writes, "I had never consciously invoked Julian, but her anchorhold, dimly lit, with a fireplace at one end and a cat, was in my mind's eye a real place, and a safe place." For the rest of Lent and for many weeks beyond, I listened for the echoes of that cell, hearing their resonance hundreds of years later in the morning quiet that filled my cabin—not quite a cell, but a small space, a hermitage of sorts, where I lived with a cat of my own and with a longing for such a love to permeate me, to be revealed through me.

## Julian's Enclosure

When they closed the door,
watching through the window
as she set down her armful
of belongings,
I wonder if some thought
she would go mad
never leaving that small space.

When they closed the door,
I wonder if she breathed
a sigh of relief,
knowing how she finally had
everything she needed,
how she had already been taken
by the God who loves small things.

ent was quite a season for reading this year. Another devoured book was China Galland's *Longing for Darkness,* her account of a ten-year journey to find female faces of the divine. China writes of how her quest led her to the Black Madonna.

In churches and shrines across Europe and in other places around the world, hundreds of statues and paintings of Mary, the mother of Jesus, depict her as dark- or black-skinned. Some of these depictions, China observes, have darkened from the smoke of church candles and incense or because they were carved out of wood whose color has deepened over time. Some, however, were intentionally created dark. China tells of her pilgrimage to several of the black madonnas, including the ones in Einsiedeln, Sweden, and Czestochowa, Poland, where the Black Madonna is the patron saint of the Solidarity movement. China found herself fascinated by the dark images and became convinced that their darkness conveys a powerful message. "This is a multivalent darkness," she writes. "This is the darkness of ancient wisdom, of people of color, of space, of the womb, of the earth, of the unknown, of sorrow, of the imagination, the darkness of death, of the human heart, of the unconscious, of the darkness beyond light, of matter, of the descent of the body, of the shadow of the Most High."

In a house in San Antonio, Texas, on the way to visit another Black Madonna, China encountered an icon of the Madre de los Desaparecidos—the Mother of the Disappeared. Painted by contemporary iconographer Robert Lentz, this dark-skinned madre holds a crown of thorns. Trees of El Salvador stand in the background, and smudged onto a corner of the painting is a handprint dripping with white paint, a sign of one of the death squads in Central America. This madre knows the sorrows of those whose loved ones have been taken from them, the grief of those mourning the disappeared ones who were imprisoned, tortured, and sometimes killed by government soldiers. Contemplating this dark madonna, China began to see Mary not as a passive figure but as a woman like these madres, who banded together and acted and protested and searched for their children and cried out for justice and sometimes became *desaparecidas* themselves.

## Bidding the Black Madonna

When the glare obscures our vision,
come to us from darkness hidden,
tendering your words of soothing,
smoothing down the shards of day.

And in the nights where violence rages,
touch the wounds of souls courageous
who wage their peace with open hands,
dancing where the shadows play.

now that I am not serving a congregation, I have the freedom to visit other churches on Sunday mornings. I enjoy the opportunity to choose where I go, but I am finding the search for a church community discouraging. I don't expect a place that perfectly fits my needs, but I long for a community whose openness and diversity beckon me to pour my heart into it. That's not what I find most Sundays. My sense of disconnection is deepened by my frustration with the language I often encounter in worship, language that is jarringly exclusive or sometimes just flat.

Sitting in church this morning, something snaps. I fight the impulse to leave, then wonder why I'm fighting. I finally slip out during the final hymn and come home exhausted and sad.

All night, the sound of things snapping echoes through my head. I imagine broken twigs scattered on the ground. I wish for a diviner who could make sense of their jumbled pattern. Or for a cartographer to turn them into a map that would point me toward the community for which I long.

Later I go outside, gather some twigs, and begin to paint them. I choose vivid colors, forming stripes and dots, working patterns into the bark. I salvage the map of Orlando I got when I moved here. I just recently retired it because I couldn't always find the right tattered piece when I needed it. I lay the twigs on top of a shred of the map and begin to lash the colorful sticks together with thick thread, thinking about bridges and boardwalks. I leave it, unfinished, on a shelf. Only later do I realize it looks like a raft.

When I cannot find the words
and when I will not;
when solitude is my only offering
and silence takes up its lodgings
in my soul;
when anger is my invocation
and breaking my benediction,
O God,
hear my prayer.

n my search for a more imaginative liturgical language, I've found that the use of inclusive language is no guarantee I won't leave a worship service hungry. Much of what passes for inclusive language would more rightly be called nonexclusive language, in that the use of gender-neutral names for God and humanity does not lift up one name and image to the exclusion of others. Yet language that is only gender-neutral, though it represents a critical step, only goes so far. When it does not draw on the wide array of images and names for God present in Scripture, in tradition, and in our experience, it is not completely inclusive. To the extent that language offers a wide vocabulary for speaking of God and of humans, it is truly inclusive.

The evolution of language within the church tends to be slow and awkward. In the struggle to find our way toward a more encompassing language, we have often lost the beauty and poetry that emerge in speaking of the particular. It is this that starves me in the sanctuary as much as anything: that the words we choose for worship, whether using exclusive or nonexclusive language, are so often thin.

As I have struggled with my own use of language, I have fallen in love with the work of a woman named Janet Morley. A British author who has written and edited several collections of prayers, including her stunning *All Desires Known*, Janet writes prayers that take a quantum leap toward inclusivity. She has not deleted gender but has woven it into her prayers without sacrificing the beauty of the language. The prayers and litanies which emerge from her pen are textured and rich and sensual.

I want to stretch myself that way. I long to plow the language, finding words buried and fertile in the dark, dark earth. I want to write prayers like pomegranates, fat and seedy, the color of blood, tangy and sweet, replete with mystery. I want to craft prayers that surprise and stun, that invite and welcome, that uncover and lay bare, that delight and entice; prayers that awaken my eyes and ears and other senses, my heart and soul, peeling back the layers that have become deadened by so many lifeless prayers. I long for prayers that comfort and challenge, that call me home and feed me and send me on my way.

Thou who created the world
with a word,
hear me:
when I am hungering
for a language I have not found,
when I am thirsting
for phrases yet to be born,
when the words I have heard
turn to ash in my ear
and what I have uttered
becomes dust in my mouth,
quiet me
to hear you
speaking the words
that will create the world again.

A number of feminist authors have written of the need to construct a usable past, to piece together the fragments of women's history in an attempt to imagine what the past really looked like. In her book *At the Root of This Longing*, Carol Lee Flinders describes this usable past as "a frame of reference that made my personal history comprehensible. A garment that fit." In the Christian tradition, one way we do this is by searching for the voices and stories that are present but often forgotten. Plowing the Scriptures for the pieces and fragments, for the stories and suggestions of women's presence, even when their names have not been recorded; searching the tradition for women's words, visions, rituals, tales: this is how we re-member.

But remembering is not our final task, for there are stories we will never find, no matter how many times we search the sacred texts. I think it was Marcia Falk who wrote, "What we cannot remember, we must imagine." And so we read between the lines, listening beneath the layers of suppression and neglect to hear the chorus of voices where we were told there was only silence.

I remember the goosebumps I got when I first heard how the names of the martyrs and the disappeared ones are called in Central America and South America. The voices of those listening ring out, after each name, "Presente!" Present. They are here. Remembered. Their silencing, their disappearance, their death will not wipe out their memory, will not erase their lives.

I think of the women and want to cry out, *they are here, they are here, they are here.*

## The Memory of Stars

Outside my window it is full day.
The sun slants across my bed
where the cat named Ezekiel lies,
his white spots warm,
his black spots hot.
Last night we lay with
noses pointed toward the sky,
one of us, at least, watching
the stars that made it
past the glare of city lights.

Stretched out beside Zeke
in the light of day,
I think of the women,
those whose stories were erased
like distant stars swallowed up
by the morning sky.
We soak up their energy
the way Zeke takes in the sun,
yet fail to see the lights
that burn through the day.

I think of how the Scriptures
are like the sky at twilight,
the tradition like the sky at dusk:
one revealing some pinpoints
of light,
the other revealing more.

I long for full night,
for a brilliant darkness
where we don't have to work
so hard to see
how they are always there, blazing,
holding up their half of the sky.

**I** left on a trip to Toronto during the summer of the Florida fires. For days the flames had raged as the temperatures increased and the heavens withheld their rains. I looked through my cabin window late one afternoon and joyously thought, "It's raining!" I looked closer and realized it was smoke. I went outside and scanned the shoreline, fully expecting to see flames. All I saw was a landscape covered by a smoky haze. The fires were still miles away from my doorstep, but I found it small comfort to live in the woods in those days.

After packing my bags for my Toronto trip, I packed a box of my treasures and gave my boyfriend Paul a list of what I wanted saved in the event the fires threatened the cabin. First on the list was my cat Zeke; after that, the treasure-filled fire box, which contained photographs, old family Bibles, and my flute. Then the wood sculptures that Paul had carved, my cassock and alb that friends from St. Luke's had given me, my guitar. If there was time, the artwork on the walls. Making the list, I thought about what I considered important. With the exception of Zeke, none of this was essential. I told Paul repeatedly that none of the possessions warranted risking life or limb.

As I boarded the plane for Toronto and began to ascend toward a clearer clime, concern tugged at me even as relief washed over me. Although few homes had burned in the vast expanse of wildfire, I found it difficult to ponder the devastation that had seared the land. Yet I knew, too, that the earth would make use of the ash and that new green shoots would emerge again.

Blessed are you, O God,
in whom nothing is wasted.
You salvage the remnant,
the scrap, the shred.
You bless what is left
from the consuming fire, the devouring flood,
the shearing wind, the shifting earth.
All that remains
returns to you
and is reborn from you.

Blessed are you, O God,
who brings life from the earth
and will return it to earth
once again.

THE EARTH WOULD MAKE
USE OF THE ASH AND
green
shoots
WOULD EMERGE AGAIN

*And early in the morning Jesus came walking toward them*

*on the sea. But when the disciples saw him walking on the sea,*

*they were terrified, saying, "It is a ghost!" And they cried*

*out in fear. But immediately Jesus spoke to them and said,*

*"Take heart, it is I; do not be afraid."*

*Peter answered him, "Lord, if it is you, command me to come*

*to you on the water." He said, "Come." So Peter got out*

*of the boat, started walking on the water, and came toward Jesus.*

*But when he noticed the strong wind, he became frightened,*

*and beginning to sink, he cried out, "Lord, save me!"*

*Jesus immediately reached out his hand and caught him, saying*

*to him, "You of little faith, why did you doubt?"*

—MATTHEW 14:25–31

It isn't a Lenten text, but I found myself thinking about it as I pondered this monotype print. I began to imagine a different figure, just beyond the margins of the ink, hearing the voice that called across those waves . . .

## The Woman Who Walked on Water

She couldn't remember
how long she had been riding
so low in the water,
waves lapping over the edges
of the vessel that defined her limits.
And she couldn't recall
at what point the oars had become
one with her hands,
their pattern ingrained on her palms.

It was not premeditated,
but when she heard that voice
calling over the water,
she let the oars slip
into the darkness
and she set off across the waves.

*You have kept count of my tossings; put my tears in your bottle.*

*Are they not in your record?*

—PSALM 56:8

i am fascinated by a hand-blown Egyptian tear jar that came into my keeping several years ago. It is a fragile thing, colored a watery blue with a ribbon of white that looks like foam on the ocean. Legend has it that the one who fills the jar with her tears will be given her heart's desire. At the 1995 International United Methodist Clergywomen's Consultation in Atlanta, women greeted us at one of the worship services with baskets of tear jars, inviting us to choose one as we entered into worship. I remember little of that worship service except that it had to do with grieving and that I ached from the inside out. I remember the tear jars so fragile and delicate in the hands of these strong women, remember the hands of many colors holding the jars of many hues. I have never wept into it but I love the story, love knowing that tears—the wrenching sweating of our souls—can become a thing of beauty and power when they are gathered together, when they are honored and blessed.

Holding the tear jar in my hand, I think of Luke's account of a woman with an alabaster jar of perfume who anoints Jesus, who weeps onto his feet and dries them with her hair (Luke 7:36–50). It is an act of profound sorrow and celebration mixed. No words are ascribed to her in the text, but her gesture speaks volumes. An uninvited presence, she comes from beyond the boundaries of the table to enact a word of lamentation, repentance, and devotion. In her silence she speaks as no one else dares.

The woman who anoints Jesus' feet embodies the sort of lamentation that Maria Harris addresses in her book *Women and Teaching*. Writing about mourning, Maria remarks that "for many women it is the beginning of speech." Our mourning compels us to name our sorrows, to name our losses, to name our wounds inflicted and received. Our grieving beckons us, too, to name our causes for joy, to name our dreams and longings. Our mourning invites us beyond our own heart's desires into the heart of a world as fragile as glass, as easily broken, and brimming with the promise of healing.

## Blessing of the Tears

That I may be filled with them.
That I may be emptied by them.

That they may challenge
my silence.
That they may lead me
to speech.

That I may name each one.
That I may be named by each one.

That they may teach me
of my sorrow.
That they may lead me
to my strength.

In writing about mourning, Maria Harris speaks to the importance of the ways that mourning takes place within a community. She writes, "What rituals of mourning need not be is sad or solemn. Indeed, beyond song and silence, they can go on to include laughter and dance. Anyone who has ever been to an Irish wake knows that." The season of Lent invites us to embrace that tension. In *The Handbook of the Christian Year,* the authors point out that the Sundays in Lent are "little Easters," possessing a character all their own. "It is not enough that these Sundays be like other Sundays, glorious as any Lord's Day," the writers caution. "Neither is it enough to treat these Sundays as if Lent were simply one long Holy Week, concentrating on the suffering and death of Christ, as if we could ignore for even a single Lord's Day the fact of the risen, living Christ in our midst."

I think of how some of my fondest memories have arisen from times of sorrow: food-laden family gatherings after a funeral, Linda and Lesley feeding me during a sad evening, Karen showing up on my doorstep with a bottle of wine on a night of bad news. Those who grace us in our grieving carry resurrection within them, giving flesh to the Wisdom born from the meeting of sorrow and joy.

## Benedictus

In your leaving
we say peace.
With the last light of you dying
we say peace.
And where there is no peace
we say peace
in the hope it will rest in our bones.

In your going
we say joy.
With the last breath of you leaving
we say joy.
And where there is no joy
we say joy
in the hope it will dwell in our flesh.

In your departing
we say love.
With the earth taking you in
we say love.
And where there is no love
we say love
in the hope it will come to our souls.

In
Wisdom's
Path

Lent

# PALM SUNDAY

*As Jesus rode along, people kept spreading their cloaks on the road. As he was now approaching the path down from the Mount of Olives, the whole multitude of the disciples began to praise God joyfully with a loud voice for all the deeds of power that they had seen, saying, "Blessed is the king who comes in the name of the Lord! Peace in heaven, and glory in the highest heaven!" Some of the Pharisees in the crowd said to him, "Teacher, order your disciples to stop." He answered, "I tell you, if these were silent, the stones would shout out."*

—Luke 19:36–40

S tands of palmetto trees inhabit the woods around my cabin. They remind me of the palmettos we had in the woods behind the house where I grew up. I remember my father cutting palmetto fronds for Palm Sunday processions at church, the full fronds a stark contrast to the single palm strand handed to me in Palm Sunday services of more recent years. The scrap of palm strikes me as a thin reminder of what must have lined the road into Jerusalem that day. More than an effort to conserve time or foliage, it seems a symptom of our own reserve, of our reluctance to lavish greetings upon the sacred when it appears in our midst.

While in Alaska several years ago, I picked up a book called *Leaf and Bone: African Praise-Poems,* edited by Judith Gleason. A form of oral literature peculiar to Africa, praise-poems are highly refined, formulaic word creations which a person works a lifetime to master. Such poems are crafted for the naming of a child, the initiation of a young person into adulthood, the honoring of a host, the recognition of a spirit, the revering of a god. Judith includes poems in praise of clans, hunters, animals, earth, and rain, as well as lamentations by women.

The poems remind me of Celtic blessings, which richly acknowledge the ways that the sacred permeates all of life. Every object, every action, every encounter becomes an opportunity to remember one's connection with God. They remind me, too, of St. Francis's "Canticle to the Sun," in which he acknowledges elements of creation as kin to him.

The praise–poems of Gleason's book reawakened my eyes and ears to the poetry of praise. With words that are lavish, drenching, and very particular, they reminded me of the multitude of ways in which we can acknowledge the spark of the divine in creation and can bless the Creator whose fingerprints are scattered across the earth.

70

In
Wisdom's
Path

Lent

Praise to the Word,
to the One who carries
silence within him,
who speaks with hands
touching what taboo had claimed,
who speaks with feet
crossing lines the law had drawn,
who speaks with belly
full of the feasts
shared with sinners,
who speaks with eyes
taking into his gaze

those whom others had looked past,
looked over,
looked through.

Praise to the Word
whose silence causes
men to listen
women to rise
children to see visions
old ones to dream
stones to cry out
praise  praise  praise.

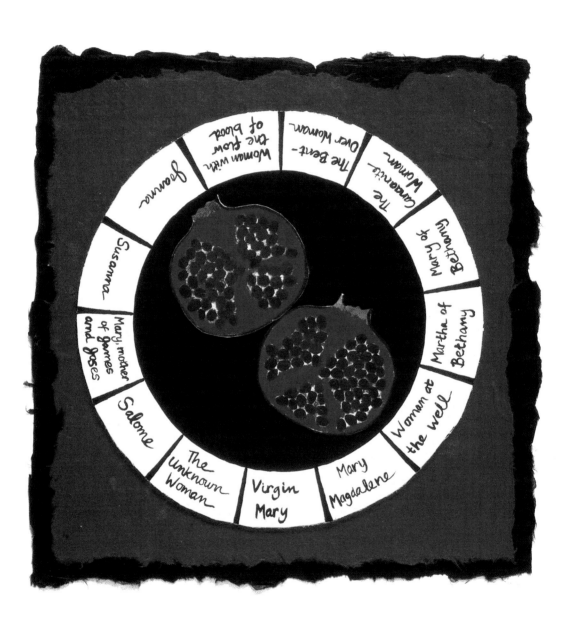

# HOLY WEEK: HOLY THURSDAY

*When the hour came, he took his place at the table, and the apostles with him. He said to them, "I have eagerly desired to eat this Passover with you before I suffer; for I tell you, I will not eat it until it is fulfilled in the kingdom of God."*

—LUKE 22:14–16

the red in this image provides the only spot of color in the artwork for this season. That's what the women around Jesus are for me in these stark days: colorful and vivid and passionate in the ways they encounter and accompany him, especially as they anoint him, touch him, tend him with compassion and courage in his final days. And though the Gospels bear witness to their companioning of Jesus in his journey toward the cross, the women are mysteriously absent from the text of the Last Supper. Yet I think they must have feasted somewhere, those women whom Jesus touched and who touched him in turn; somewhere they remembered and prepared for what lay ahead.

## Eucharista

We give great thanks for you
who gave your body and blood
to give him birth,
who sustained him in his growing,
who traveled the path with him,
who supported him
from your own resources.

We give great thanks for you
who reached to him for healing,
who challenged him with questions,
who shared your table with him,
who claimed your place at his.

We give great thanks for you
who drank in every word,
who told out his good news,
who touched him in his leaving,
who walked with him toward death.

And so,
with thanksgiving and celebration,
we praise you:
you who found
the stones of your life
turned to bread by him,
we remember you.

You who found
your bitter cup
turned to wine by him,
we remember you.

You whose names
have been lost to the winds,
whose stories
have been turned to scraps,
whose voices
echo through the ages
and beckon us to listen,
we give thanks
and we remember you.

73

In
Wisdom's
Path

Lent

# HOLY WEEK: GOOD FRIDAY

## (On the Way to the Cross)

As they led Jesus away, they seized a man, Simon of Cyrene,

who was coming from the country, and they laid the cross on him,

and made him carry it behind Jesus. A great number of

the people followed him, and among them were women who were

beating their breasts and wailing for him. But Jesus turned to them

and said, "Daughters of Jerusalem, do not weep for me,

but weep for yourselves and for your children. For the days are

surely coming when they will say, 'Blessed are the barren,

and the wombs that never bore, and the breasts that never nursed.'

Then they will begin to say to the mountains, 'Fall on us';

and to the hills, 'Cover us.' For if they do this when the wood is

green, what will happen when it is dry?"

—LUKE 23:26–31

This piece started out as a monotype print, but I reverted to collage to better depict what I held in my mind's eye. This image captures the women at the moment before Jesus turns to address them. We have no record of any response they might have made to his searing words.

The women may have been professional mourners, just doing their job as Jesus walked the Way of Sorrows. It's also possible that they had been followers of Jesus during his life who now followed him toward his death, their voices crying out in grief and lamentation. Regardless of their identity, Jesus' comments seem designed to bring them up short. I wonder what thoughts flashed through their minds, what fears or hopes stirred in their threatened wombs and breasts.

## The Green Wood Chant

Tell out, my soul,
what my eyes have seen
while the tree is strong
and the wood is green.

When the tree grows old
and the wood is dry,
we will bow our heads
and we'll raise our cry.

Yet we'll hold the fire,
and we'll hold the ash,
and we'll hold your life
till your sorrows pass;

and we'll place the dust
in the fertile ground,
and we'll wait to see
what comes around.

# HOLY WEEK: GOOD FRIDAY
## (At the Cross)

When it was noon, darkness came over the whole land until three in
the afternoon. At three o'clock Jesus cried out with a loud voice,
"Eloi, Eloi, lema sabachthani?" which means, "My God, my
God, why have you forsaken me?" When some of the bystanders
heard it, they said, "Listen, he is calling for Elijah."
And someone ran, filled a sponge with sour wine, put it on a stick,
and gave it to him to drink, saying, "Wait, let us see whether
Elijah will come to take him down." Then Jesus gave a loud cry
and breathed his last. And the curtain of the temple was
torn in two, from top to bottom. Now when the centurion, who stood
facing him, saw that in this way he breathed his last, he said,
"Truly this man was God's Son!"

There were also women looking on from a distance; among them
were Mary Magdalene, and Mary the mother of James
the younger and of Joses, and Salome. These used to follow him
and provided for him when he was in Galilee; and there were many
other women who had come up with him to Jerusalem.

—MARK 15:33–41

## Friday from Noon till Three
### (The Magdalene's Lament)

Perhaps they wondered
why I was not surprised
when they told of how
the curtain had been torn.

But I had known
the exact moment of the rending.
It started at my heart
and did not stop
until it had reached my womb,
and the holy of holies
lay bare and bleeding
with a gash
no one else could see.

On Easter weekend Paul and I are in Asheville, North Carolina: my haven, my mecca. We stay with Sandra, whose home I have come to think of as the House of Good Food and Cheer. We spend much of our visit eating and sitting on Sandra's deck. Sandra and I go hiking. Paul spends time gathering leaves, then spreads them in front of the fireplace, sitting with a tree book in hand as he identifies them one by one. He points out birds to Sandra that she had not known were her neighbors.

On Holy Saturday the three of us plant two flame azaleas on the slope beside Sandra's house. We take turns digging into the resistant earth. Sandra unwraps the azaleas and gingerly places them in their holes. We cover them and watch as she waters them for the first time. She names them Paul and Jan. Their underground work begins.

Planting seems appropriate for this day. I think of other digging done on this day years ago—of burying my cat Jake one sunny Easter eve, then immediately driving to a cemetery where I presided at the graveside service of a child who had been born just days earlier. I remember standing at that grave and acknowledging how few words fit the occasion. To the small group of mourners I spoke of others who had waited on this same day two millennia earlier, clinging to one another in the aftermath of death. There are few words of comfort for this day—just a waiting, a holding of the breath in the darkness between death and resurrection.

Thou
who breathed in the womb,
who dwelled in the tomb,
mercy, have mercy
on us who wait.

# EASTER

## WALKING OUT OF THE WOUND

*Does Wisdom not call meanwhile?*
*Does Discernment not lift up her voice?*
*On the hilltop, on the road, at the crossways,*
*she takes her stand; beside the gates of the*
*city, at the approaches to the gates she cries*
*aloud. . . . "Listen, I have serious things*
*to tell you, from my lips come honest words."*

—Proverbs 8:1—3, 6 (JB)

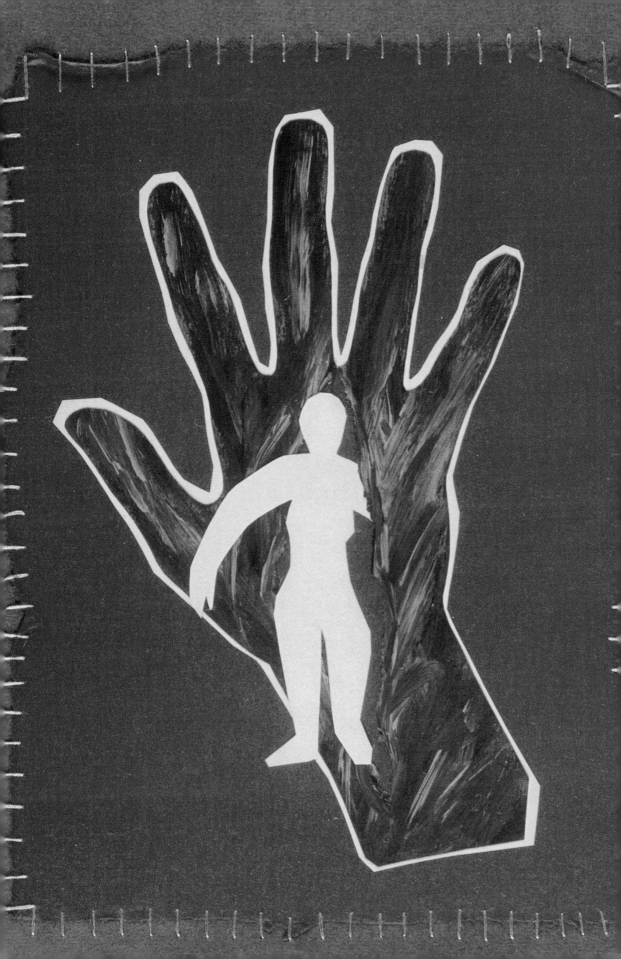

*A woman stands in a garden* weeping beside an open, empty tomb. Turning around, she sees but does not recognize the beloved man whose body she seeks. "Woman, why are you weeping?" he asks her. Thinking him to be the gardener, she replies, "Sir, if you have carried him away, tell me where you have laid him, and I will take him away." Only when Jesus calls Mary Magdalene by name does she recognize who stands before her.

Evidently Mary reaches out to touch her beloved teacher and friend, for Jesus' next words to her are a command to not hold on to him because he has not yet ascended to God. For a long time I found Jesus' words to Mary harsh, rubbing salt into the wound of her sorrow over his horrible death, snatching away her elation at seeing him living and breathing before her. Then I happened upon Elisabeth Moltmann-Wendel's discussion of this passage in her book *The Women around Jesus* where she writes, "I would prefer to translate the words 'Don't touch me' like this: 'Grow up, be mature! Accept the grief of parting.'" Standing before Jesus, Mary is a wounded woman. Marked by her loss and grief, she still carries the scars of the wounds that Jesus had healed long ago. Yet Jesus knows it is time for Mary to let go, to allow the form of their relationship to change, and to tell the story of what she has seen. In choosing to leave the garden and proclaim what has happened, Mary begins to walk out of her wounds.

In working with abused women and men, in ministering as a church pastor, in listening to my friends, and in working on my own wounds, I have learned that many of us carry injuries we bear no responsibility for receiving. We carry wounds, too, that bear the mark of our own hand, whether intentional or unintentional. I believe that, regardless of the source of the wounds, we do have a responsibility to seek their healing. They may long plague us, but God beckons us in due season to cease to cling to them lest we remain forever victimized. There comes a time when we must choose whether to remain weeping at the tomb or to let go and tell what we have seen.

Mary's healing begins as she walks away from the tomb and goes to tell the others what she has seen. Our healing, too, comes in proclamation, in finding words that will become a pathway out of our wounds. In her book *Sisters of the Yam,* bell hooks shares the words of a student of hers, engaged in her own process of recovery. "Healing occurs through testimony," she said, "through gathering together everything available to you and reconciling." Hundreds of years earlier, the desert father Abba Poemen said it another way: "Teach your mouth to say that which you have in your heart."

The ways we choose to find our words, tell our stories, offer our testimonies, and walk out of our wounds are myriad. No matter how it comes, each word draws us into the footsteps of Wisdom, who calls out from the hilltop, who lifts her voice on the road, who takes her stand at the crossways, who cries aloud at the city gates, speaking the truth of what she knows.

*Easter*

everal years ago. a friend who had begun to recover memories of being sexually abused as a child invited me to participate in a service of healing. She asked me to write a prayer of confession as a contribution to the service. I agreed but puzzled over how to write about confession in this context. She had not instigated the harm done to her: what had she to confess?

I wrote this prayer as I sat at her kitchen table one afternoon. watching her bake bread. As I shared the prayer at her service the next day. I spoke of my belief that at the heart of confession lies the power to name: not simply to name what we have done wrong but to name what has been done to us and to name our own struggles to claim responsibility for our healing. I said that I believe such healing comes through small acts that work as leaven in our lives: through graced moments such as baking and breaking bread together. sharing tea. taking walks. and breaking the silence one word at a time.

## Prayer of Confession

God of compassion,
we acknowledge the times
we have lived too long
with the words that others have put
into our mouths,
with the pain they have written
onto our bodies,
with the terror they have burned
into our hearts,
with the shame they have inscribed
onto our souls.
We know the times we have clung
to sackcloth not of our making,
when we have lived
clothed in weariness,
cloaked with anger,
and enshrouded by sorrow.
We grieve the occasions
when we have lived with alienation
rather than association,
when we have sought isolation
rather than consolation,
when our wounds within
have shut others out.
We confess our fear of the dark
and our uncertainty of the light.

Yet you have placed within us, God,
a longing for survival,
a hunger for your wholeness,
a yearning for your comfort,
and a hope for all our healing.
Bless our mouths
to name our wounds,
that we may not fear them;
our bodies,
that we may cherish them;
our hearts, that we may delight
in their longings,
and our souls, that we may trust
the wisdom of the stories they hold.
Grant us the courage
to be touched by you,
that when our days of weeping
are done,
we may wear your garments
of gladness,
see one another in the light
of your love,
and stand together in the power
of your resurrection.
In the name of the risen Christ,
we pray. Amen.

*In the beginning when God created the heavens and the earth, the earth was a formless void and darkness covered the face of the deep, while a wind from God swept over the face of the waters. Then God said . . .*

—Genesis 1:1–3a

According to Genesis, the world begins with a word. Speech gives way to substance and forms every living thing. I wonder if this was the first time God spoke. And I wonder if God began to create because God longed to hear her own voice, to see it take form and flesh in the unfolding of the world.

Elie Wiesel, who survived the Holocaust and has spent the rest of his life turning its horrors into stories, says that God created people because God loves stories. We are the vessels of God's voice, her words blowing through us, bidding us to tell the tales that only we can speak.

Your wind
over my waters;

your light
in my dark;

your seas
in my earth;

your seasons
in my sky;

your beasts
in my deep;

your breath
in my flesh:

create, O God,
from my wakening depths.

ome time ago I went through a period of feeling constrained in the ways I could express myself. In my vocation and in my personal life, I wrestled with how to allow the images and ideas and longings within me to find voice in the world around me. My inner struggle manifested itself physically as a viselike grip on my throat, a tightness that lasted for days at a time and left me feeling bruised.

I began to understand the tightness as a visitor that had come to tell me I wasn't giving voice to something in my life. As I worked to break the silences I kept, its grip began to loosen, but it still takes hold from time to time. One day, during a session with my spiritual director, I lamented how long it was taking to completely rid myself of it. "The knot in your throat didn't weave itself in a short time, Jan," she reminded me. "It's not going to unravel all at once."

This image emerged as I began to think of knots and webs, of untangling and loosing, of what it takes to unweave the strands of a pattern that doesn't work. I have heard people speak of storytelling as a weaving of words, but sometimes the storyteller speaks to set them free, to unbind the words that have stayed tangled too long, to unwind the knotted phrases before they choke her to death.

Unwrapping
unwinding
untangling
unbinding

unraveling
unweaving
unknotting
unwebbing

waking up
calling forth
setting free
resurrecting:
the ways that you loosen
my Lazarus tongue.

Of the essays contained in the powerful collection that Audre Lorde published under the title *Sister Outsider,* the one I return to most frequently is the one she called "The Transformation of Silence into Language and Action." Audre tells of a conversation she had with her daughter in the course of writing this essay, which she delivered at the Modern Language Association's "Lesbian and Literature Panel" in 1977. Listening to her mother speak of her fears connected with turning her silence into speech, hearing her reflect on the dangers of self-revelation that accompany such speaking, Audre's daughter said to her, "Tell them about how you're never really a whole person if you remain silent, because there's always that one little piece inside you that wants to be spoken out, and if you keep ignoring it, it gets madder and madder and hotter and hotter, and if you don't speak it out one day it will just up and punch you in the mouth from the inside."

## Speaking of Audre

Your silence will not protect you,
you said.
But neither will our speech.
Every word is a stripping,
a laying bare,
divesting ourselves of every security
we thought our unspeaking would give us.

Learning to speak
means learning
that our words will not protect us, either,
but that every syllable can become a solace,
every utterance a strength,
every phrase a prayer for courage
to say the burning
in our souls.

Another of my favorite essays in Audre Lorde's book *Sister Outsider* is "Poetry Is Not a Luxury." She writes of poetry as illumination, as light that reveals our ideas, hopes, and dreams. Poetry draws into the light of day the deep, hidden, dark place inside us where possibility and creativity and power dwell. When poetry sheds such light, she writes, it is not a luxury, not a frivolous activity that takes us away from our "real" work. "It is a vital necessity of our existence," Audre writes. "It forms the quality of the light within which we predicate our hopes and dreams toward survival and change, first made into language, then into idea, then into more tangible action. Poetry is the way we help give name to the nameless so it can be thought. The farthest horizons of our hopes and fears are cobbled by our poems, carved from the rock experiences of our daily lives."

While poetry does this in ways particular to the written word, other forms of artistry, too, shed light on the recesses of power we contain within us. In the face of those depths that we sometimes tremble to touch, creative expression offers a form, a language for speaking the unspeakable in our lives.

Audre's chapter title has become something of a mantra, a charm when doubts about the value of creativity begin to arise from within me or beyond me. *Not a luxury,* I repeat to myself. To be sure, no artistic discipline is wholly immune to flights of self-indulgence. But I think of Etty Hillesum crafting her words as the Nazis marched into Holland, of Guatemalan poet Julia Esquivel stringing together her words like pearls on the aching and bloody tendon that connects her with her homeland, of the women and men and children who remember their beloved dead as they stitch each memory into yet another panel of the Names Project AIDS Memorial Quilt. *Not a luxury.* I think of the farmworker children in nearby Apopka who received cameras to take pictures of their community and who bore powerful photographic witness to their lives. *Not a luxury.* I think of folk singers who have given voice to generations of struggle and hope. *Not a luxury.* I think of the writers, visual artists, musicians, dancers whose lifeblood has sustained me, those creative souls who for countless people have made the difference between wholeness and despair and sometimes between life and death, and I know that what they give is *not a luxury, not a luxury, not a luxury.*

There are days
when books are the only bread
for those who hunger,
and those who thirst
have only songs
to slake their aching tongues.

And there are nights
when those who have
lost their voice
find it in the contours of a canvas,
and poetry is the only vessel
for holding all the pain.

May you, Creator God,
bless those whose acts of art
offer a beacon in the shadows,
a garden in the desert,
a way out of the wilderness,
and a table for the feast.

NANCY MAIRS·TERRY
TEMPEST WILLIAMS·
KATHLEEN NORRIS·JOY
HARJO·JANET MORLEY·
bell hooks·CARTER
HEYWARD·JULIA CAM-
ERON·JULIAN OF NOR-
WICH·ANNIE DILLARD·
TONI MORRISON·MEIN-
RAD CRAIGHEAD·ISABEL
ALLENDE·MARGE PIERCY·
MADELEINE L'ENGLE·ETTY
HILLESUM·JULIA ESQUIVEL

**S**oon after I moved to Orlando, an advertisement for an exhibit of artists' books at the art museum in Ormond Beach captured my attention. On a day off I drove to the beach and found myself enchanted as I browsed through the exhibit, titled "The Book Unbound." As an artist and writer, I was astounded that I had never before encountered this medium, in which books become art forms through the use of nontraditional bindings, papers, and formats. A world had opened before me. I sent off for information from several places in the United States that deal in the book arts. Browsing through one catalog I received, I came across an announcement for a book that used a font whose letters were based on the shape of the bones of birds.

Much later, mulling over questions of words and language as I walked the grounds of San Pedro one afternoon, I remembered the bird-boned letters which the font designer had created. I began to ponder what it would look like to design letters based on the shape of the veins of women. I wondered how words would look if we could see the ways that women had fashioned them from broken and mended hearts, from blood vessels that coursed with the stories of their lives, from arteries that fed throats straining to tell the truth of their souls. I thought of women writers whose words had rescued me in the desert of language, whose letters and syllables coursed through my blood, who kept my heart pumping with their insistent drumming, *You can speak, you can speak, you can speak.*

In the vein
and in the vessel,
in the marrow
of the bone,
in the chambers
of the heart,
in the waters
of the womb;

in the teeth
and in the tongue,
in the pounding
of the blood,
you speak
a new creation
in the flesh
becoming word.

In
Wisdom's
Path

*Easter*

*Poems can't be translated; they can at best be approximated in a different language. In a poem the language counts as much as the message. God is the poet. If we want to know what God says in a tomato, we must look at a tomato, feel it, smell it, bite into it, have the juice and seeds squirt all over us when it pops. We must savor it and learn this tomato poem "by heart." But what God must say can't be exhausted in tomato language. So, God gives us lemons and speaks in Lemonese. Living by the Word means learning God's languages, one by one, a lifetime long.*

—BROTHER DAVID STEINDL-RAST,

*GRATEFULNESS, THE HEART OF PRAYER*

I was led to this quote by Father Robert, one of the friars who live at San Pedro. Speaking at an Audire instructional weekend, he borrowed from these words, and I found my imagination immediately captivated. I suppose this stands as one of the reasons I turn to visual art: words can't contain it all, and not even images can contain it all, how the sacred looks, sounds, feels, smells, tastes. But I think God longs for us to dive in, to be willing to get messy, to let the trying tickle our tongues and trickle down our chins.

In this
ardent, struggling groping
in the garden of your words,
let me see you
standing in the shadows,
offering your fruit
from dripping hands;

let me hear you
laughing as I revel
in this dribbling, riotous mess;

let me know your touch
as you clean me up,
leaving a seed
still on my tongue.

*Your lips distill nectar, my bride; honey and milk*

*are under your tongue; the scent of your garments is like*

*the scent of Lebanon.*

—SONG OF SONGS 4:11

I didn't grow up with the Song of Songs. I knew it was there in the Bible, encountered it a time or two in my Genesis-to-Revelation read-throughs of the Scriptures in younger years. But I never heard it preached, never discussed it in a Bible study group, never talked about it in Sunday school. As with the book of Revelation, which is graphic in another way, the church largely shrouded the Song's potent images in silence, leaving its treasures to those who undertook a solitary journey through its chapters.

What's there is enticing, erotic, poetic, playful, frank, mysterious, and occasionally ambiguous: a combination charged enough to disconcert a church already ill at ease with matters of sexuality. Many commentators have dealt with its vivid eroticism by interpreting the Song as an allegory of God's love for Israel or Christ's love for the church. I think it is unabashedly a love story that graphically and poetically tells of the passion of a human woman and man. Yet I do not dismiss the notion that it depicts, too, the sort of longing that God has for us. I love that such language could be considered to speak of our relationship with God, that the vocabulary of lovers describes the ways that God yearns to be with us. The dance of intimacy that possesses the couple in the Song is our dance, too, as we move between desire and disappearance, yearning and turning away, losing ourselves in the beloved and looking everywhere for him, lamenting the lover's absence and lavishing her with praise.

## My Beloved Speaks and Says to Me

On a day
when I am keeping
all my quiet within me,
you say
I look like I've got a secret.

But really
I am imagining your face
when you see
the treasures I have
beneath my tongue.

n a night when the tightness visited my throat, I spent some time in prayer, my hand resting lightly at the base of my neck. An image came of a snake coiled there, curled up on my clavicle, where the energy tends to be the most intense. I had two thoughts about what kind of snake it was: that it was a python, wrapped around my vocal cords and strangling my speech, or that it was a poisonous snake, its fangs leaking a paralyzing venom.

Then I remembered that in many religious traditions, the snake holds an honored status as a symbol of wisdom. I began to think of the snake coiled at my clavicle not as harmful but as a wise messenger inviting me to pay attention to the ways I sometimes participated in my own silencing.

My pondering led me back to the story of Eve and the serpent. I think that Eve's sin lay primarily not in taking the fruit but in trying to hide her ensuing knowledge from God. When confronted by God, Eve essentially falls silent, trying to pass the blame to the serpent instead of owning up to her actions. She doesn't tell God of how she hungered, of how she longed for the wisdom of the tree, or of the terrible and wondrous knowledge that came with taking the fruit. God can smell it on her breath, can see it in her eyes, can hear it in her voice, but Eve will not say it, will not speak the truth of what she knows.

Those who live with deep attentiveness to life's unfolding know the ways that the journey brings an intimate knowledge of good and evil. I believe we are called to speak of that knowledge, to express the wisdom that emerges from our loves and our fears, from our hungers and longings, from our acts of rebellion and our passion for peace.

## Having Taken the Fruit

I remember the exact moment
that I took the fruit.
The lights of the park
called Pleasure Island
shone in the distance,
and in the place where I was trying
to recreate my world,
you offered your hand
with its enticing invitation.

Allegory only goes so far,
and I won't say
that you were a snake
or I some sinless Eve,
but in time there came
a definite leaving of some garden
with the fruit
of a terrible knowledge
lingering on my lips.

It took a long time to figure out
that my stifling silence
was not a path
back to a paradise
where I could never live.

I finally learned to listen
to the hissing in my breath
that told me the roots
of my own soul
held the healing that I sought
and that each stilted syllable
I let loose
was another leaf
on the tree of life.

*I was silent and still; I held my peace to no avail;*

*my distress grew worse, my heart became hot within me.*

*While I mused, the fire burned; then I spoke*

*with my tongue . . .*

—PSALM 39:2–3

"I've been thinking of another image for your throat," my spiritual director says one day. "I imagine a volcano in your throat, churning and boiling, all this stuff waiting to erupt." I think of a postcard my mother brought back for me from a trip to Hawai'i. A reproduction of a painting by Herb Kawainui Kane, it depicts Pele, the goddess of the volcanoes of Hawai'i. Her face is intense, her eyes piercing, her hair flowing into fiery lava streaming down the slopes of a volcano that could remain silent no longer.

I find the postcard and place it on the bookshelf beside my desk. Pele's gaze overlooks the spot where I wrestle with these words, challenging me to plumb the molten depths. It remains to be seen whether the offering I make will appease the smoldering center or will instead release its fiery flow.

God of all my dormant words,
bless me with the wisdom to befriend
the trickster in my tongue
who knows the time to speak
of the burning in my soul
before it lays me waste,
before it consumes me whole.

The same night Jacob got up and took his two wives, his two maids, and his eleven children, and crossed the ford of the Jabbok. He took them and sent them across the stream, and likewise everything that he had. Jacob was left alone; and a man wrestled with him until daybreak. When the man saw that he did not prevail against Jacob, he struck him on the hip socket; and Jacob's hip was put out of joint as he wrestled with him. Then he said, "Let me go, for the day is breaking." But Jacob said, "I will not let you go, unless you bless me." So he said to him, "What is your name?" And he said, "Jacob." Then the man said, "You shall no longer be called Jacob, but Israel, for you have striven with God and with humans, and have prevailed." Then Jacob asked him, "Please tell me your name." But he said, "Why is it that you ask my name?" And there he blessed him. So Jacob called the place Peniel, saying, "For I have seen God face to face, and yet my life is preserved." The sun rose upon him as he passed Penuel, limping because of his hip.

—Genesis 32:22–31

Every journey presents its Jabboks, places where the convergence of time and landscape provides an opportunity to wrestle in a way that will forever define us. The wrestling offers a blessing, but it offers a wounding, too, that becomes forever a part of us. Walking out of our wounds doesn't always mean that we will emerge unscathed. I think the blessing comes in drawing wisdom from our wounds, letting God trace our new names into them as we cross the river, bound for the landscape that lies beyond.

God of struggle,
come and wrestle with me.
Let us spend this night
tumbling,
strength to strength,
locked in the embrace
that names
and blesses
and shatters my frame
so as to send me
limping
across the river,
forever cleansed
of forgetting.

I come across a list of words I made years ago, words that I was chewing on at the time. I scan the list to see what words had captured my imagination. *Courage, comfort, dwell,* I read. *Tender, felicity, grace. Mystery, reverie, mystic, refuge. Wisdom, blessing, devotion, yearning.* I remember how I pondered these words, how I turned them over in my mind, how they captured my eye on the page and tugged my ear in conversation. I see *contemplate* on the list and remember David telling me how it comes from the Latin word *templum,* for temple. The templum, he said, was the place where priests discerned the future by studying the entrails of birds. A bloody word that speaks of how those who live contemplative lives seek to get to the heart of things. (The heart of thinks, I mistakenly type. It fits.)

I ponder what sort of list I would make today, what words tug at my contemplative imagination. I get out a pen and paper. Many of the words on the old list reappear as new ones rise to the surface. *Threshold,* I write. *Voice, intimate, longing. Labyrinth, testimony, passage. Shadow, passion, revelation.*

Let me bathe in your words.
Let me soak up your silence.
Let me hear your voice.
Let me enter your quiet.
Let me tell out your stories.
Let me enclose them within me.
Let me be the spaces
between phrases
where you make your home.

threshold

voice

intimate

longing

labyrinth

testimony

passage

shadow

passion

revelation

E ach book I write teaches me many things. The lessons of this one came like pulling teeth. The way these pages fall one after the other obscures the days and weeks and sometimes months that lay between them as I wrestled with the words or avoided the blank page entirely. It wasn't that I felt blocked, exactly; I could write, I just didn't always want to put on paper what was stewing in my soul. I was angry with God, mad at the church, grieving for a damaged relationship, and needing time for my spirit to catch up with all the changes that had taken place in my life. I felt about God the way I sometimes do when the intensity of a friendship necessitates a breathing space. *I know you're there,* I told God. *I just don't want to talk with you for a while.*

When we wrestle like lovers
and I let you go
to tend to my wounds
that our loving has opened;

when we argue like sisters
and I storm away
to stew in the juices
my anger has stirred;

when the force of my passion
has left me exhausted
and I turn to the silence
to gather my strength;

let me hear you still breathing
there in the shadows,
blessing the silence
and weeping my name.

As I began to wrestle with my anger during this time, I talked with my spiritual director, struggling to find words for what I sensed unfolding inside me. During one of our conversations, she spoke of perceiving shadowy places within me that had not revealed themselves to the light of my understanding or even of my awareness. She talked of how she sometimes lights a mental candle to those hidden places in herself, the action a prayer that awareness will dawn in those secret spaces. The image haunted me, and I felt the urge to make it real.

Some time later, in the lengthening hours of the night, I struck a match and touched the flame to the oil lamp that sits on the arm of the futon where I sleep. The action became an invocation, my prayers taking the shape of the flame that danced in the shadows of my darkened room. In the absence of full awareness of what was stirring within me, in the absence of words adequate to describe my struggle, I sat in the light of the burning lamp and offered what I could: my presence, with all that smoldered and shifted inside. Sitting cross-legged on the futon, I folded the quiet about myself and began to listen.

When I have no words,
thank you for hearing
the prayer in the silence,
the plea in the flame,
the benediction in my breathing,
the desire in my dark.

In the dream I sit with a gathering of people. The seats are arranged in tiers which form a nearly complete circle. At the opening in the circle stands a man clad in rich. dark vestments. His head is shaved. he wears a gold earring. and he is preaching. As he preaches. he speaks of God with stunning. beautiful words I have never heard used in a church service. I am surprised to have found myself in this place. don't know how I got there. not sure I know anyone else in the room. I lean forward. straining to catch his words. I want him to look my way. to see me. knowing that if I can catch his eye he will see in mine all the longing I have carried to hear the words he speaks. I wake with an ache.

Bless the messengers who come
in daytime,
in dreamtime,
who awaken the aching
we hold within us,
who finger the wounds
unspoken and named,
who offer the balm
that comforts and quickens.

Bless them for blessing
the emptiness in us
where stones will not satisfy
our restless hunger,
where shallow waters will not slake
our relentless thirst,
where all of our longings
cry out for welcome
and all that we dream of
beckons us on.

*If I have one duty in these times,*

*it is to bear witness.*

I cannot think about testimony, about how words help us walk out of our wounds, without thinking of Etty Hillesum. A young Dutch Jewish woman who was killed in the Holocaust, Etty left behind an astounding set of journals, published in the 1980s by J. G. Gaarlandt as *An Interrupted Life*. A friend had recommended Etty's writing when I was working on my first book, and I ended up devoting a chapter of *Sacred Journeys* to this woman who had persisted in believing in the beauty of life in the midst of the horrors of war and the systematic genocide of her people.

While writing *In Wisdom's Path*, I went away to Miami for a week to work on this section. I had taken along my copy of *An Interrupted Life* to look for the quote above, knowing I wanted to include it in this season. One evening I picked up the book to scan it for the quote and soon realized I would not be able to simply skim through Etty's words, the words that told of her work as an instructor in Russian, her intense friendships, her passionate loves, and her relationship with God, all set against the backdrop of the war which had become increasingly woven into her daily existence.

In the course of the week I reread the book cover to cover, more slowly than I had the first time. I found myself struck by the similarity of some of our questions and devastated anew by the extinguishing of the woman whom others had described as a "luminous personality." Despite having opportunities to escape, Etty remained with her people, believing she was called to be with those who were suffering. Her solidarity led her to the labor camp at Westerbork and finally to Auschwitz, where she was killed on November 30, 1943.

With her words and with her life, Etty bore stunning witness to the terror of the times, to her belief in the exquisiteness of life, and to her faith in a God present in the midst of it all. She refused to give in to the hatred that consumed many around her. Etty concludes the last entry in her journal with the words, "We must be willing to act as a balm for all wounds."

# For Etty, Who Still Walks
## on the Path of Witness

It is midday in Miami.
Esther, who bears your given name,
sets an orchid on the table outside
where I sit surrounded
by hibiscus and blooming cactus,
by poinsettia and palm.

This tropical haven
would be foreign to you,
but I think this is how
your soul must have looked:
a riot of color,
a garden of defiance
planted against the growing terror.

I long for your presence
at this table,
to tell you how your words
bore fruit
bore witness
bore hope
in the decades that followed,
how every phrase was a seed
that settled in the throats
of those struggling to speak,
how every sentence became a bloom
in the hands of those writing their way
out of the wilderness.

Bless us, Etty,
for there is still much
that cries out for witness,
and the shadows grow long,
and we need endless healing balm.

In the summer of 1996. Charlene Payne Kammerer became a bishop in the Southeastern Jurisdiction of the United Methodist Church. Along with several friends. I had gone to North Carolina for the quadrennial meeting of the jurisdictional conference in order to witness what we hoped would be the last leg of Charlene's journey to the episcopacy. Our elation at the election of this gifted pastor and leader was deepened by the fact that this was the first time that the Southeastern Jurisdiction had chosen a woman as bishop. the last jurisdiction in the United States to do so.

The clergywomen of the jurisdiction threw a party for Charlene on the night of her election. Present at the celebration was Helen Crotwell. a United Methodist minister from North Carolina. During the storytelling that took place that evening. someone told of how. prior to the jurisdictional conference of 1992. Helen had been asked to offer herself as a candidate for the episcopacy. Helen. and those who asked her. knew that the climate in the jurisdiction did not bode well for a woman candidate and that it would be a grueling process. Still. Helen felt called to accept. The conference passed without the election of a woman. A group of clergywomen from the jurisdiction sent Helen a pottery bowl and pitcher in gratitude for the way she had given herself. The bowl broke in shipping. and Helen told the clergywomen that she would not have it repaired until the jurisdiction elected a woman as bishop.

We mended the bowl that night. Helen and Charlene began. holding the bowl together as they put glue to the pieces. Others joined in. holding and gluing as the bowl took shape once again.

Later. the clergywomen of the Florida Conference held a celebration for Charlene to send her on her way to North Carolina. where she would begin her ministry as the bishop of the Western North Carolina Conference. Asked in advance to lead a ritual of anointing for Charlene. I meditated on the words of Psalm 133. where the psalmist writes.

*How very good and pleasant it is when kindred live together in unity! It is like the precious oil on the head, running down upon the beard, on the beard of Aaron, running down over the collar of his robes. It is like the dew of Hermon, which falls on the mountains of Zion. For there the Lord ordained God's blessing, life forevermore.*

As the women gathered in a circle around Charlene. I shared the psalmist's words and this blessing.

To be together on this night
is like the oil running down the beard of Aaron, yes, but . . .
it is also like the fragrant oil used by the woman who anointed Jesus' head,
 who came into the circle and claimed her place at the table;
it is like the oil used by the woman who anointed Jesus' feet,
 wept on them, and dried them with her hair, knowing how utterly
 she was loved;
it is like the oil used by the wise virgins to light their lamps,
 knowing that the bridegroom might appear for such a time as this;
it is like the life-giving oil promised to the widow of Zarephath
 by the prophet Elijah, who told her that it would not run out
 until God had washed the earth with rain;
it is like the oil kept by every woman
 in the place where she prepares her food,
 the place where she prepares what will sustain her kindred and herself;
it is like the oil that drenches the one willing to be the squeaky wheel!

We know that it is not always good and pleasant to dwell together,
and we are not always in unity, but there is healing oil.
May you know it.

We are anointed by one another and by those who have gone before us,
by those who have offered themselves for change, for transformation,
for the healing of the world.
May we remember.

In

Wisdom's

Path

Easter

# PENTECOST SUNDAY

*When the day of Pentecost had come, they were all together in one place. And suddenly from heaven there came a sound like the rush of a violent wind. . . .*

—ACTS 2:1–2a

On Pentecost Sunday this past year, I gathered with a small group of women in one of our homes. We were a varied lot, but one thing connected us: a sense of hunger for something beyond what we could find in our respective churches. None of us was ready to turn her back on the church, but we each longed for a space that more fully engaged us.

What became a group that meets monthly for conversation and ritual began on that Pentecost Sunday. We had not chosen that day because it was Pentecost, but I considered it an auspicious beginning. Bill Mallard, one of my professors at Candler School of Theology, told his students that the miracle of Pentecost was not that the people spoke in different languages but that they understood one another. This means they must have really listened to one another, must have really heard the remarkable words springing from each other's mouths. It is that gift, that miracle of listening that I hunger for in the church, where passion for our own positions and beliefs often dims our ability to truly hear one another. Sitting in that living room on the day of Pentecost, gathered with women who had created a sacred space for speaking and for hearing, I thought of how that Spirit-filled group from every nation under heaven had, for one shining moment, gotten it right.

## Pentecost

It is not the sparks
caused by our difference
that haunt me
but the brimstone
of those bent
on assimilation,
on annihilation.

I have felt the template
on my flesh,
I have seen the wounded
and the scalded,
and I am not persuaded
that if we look alike
God will love us more.

I believe God loves the languages
of those struggling to speak
the words embedded in our flesh
of every shape and hue.

And I believe God blesses
every space where we are welcomed
to speak with tongues of fire
and hear with hearts aflame.

# ORDINARY TIME

## THE DAILY WAY

*And now, my children, listen to me: happy are those who keep my ways. Hear instruction and be wise, and do not neglect it. Happy is the one who listens to me, watching daily at my gates, waiting beside my doors. For whoever finds me finds life and obtains favor from the Lord; but those who miss me injure themselves; all who hate me love death.*

—Proverbs 8:32—36

*Ordinary Time.* That long span of time, nearly half a year, between Pentecost and the first Sunday of Advent. It contains no major feast days, nothing, it would seem, to get terribly worked up about. When I served at St. Luke's, it was an awfully long stretch of wearing my green stole Sunday after Sunday.

Although some may find Ordinary Time a lackluster season, I've grown fond of it for the ways that it invites me to discover the sacred in the rhythm of unbroken dailiness. Waking, eating, reading the paper, working, playing, talking, doing laundry, doing dishes, doing errands, doing nothing at all: how is God with us in these times? *Who* is God with us in these times?

The Scriptures tell of a God who tended to show up—or, in some cases, to send angels or other divine messengers—when humans were doing nothing in particular. Abraham was sitting at the entrance of his tent in the heat of the day when three visitors arrived to tell him that Sarah would soon be a mother. The unnamed wife of Manoah was sitting in a field when an angel came to tell her she would give birth to a son named Samson. Moses was leading a flock of sheep when he encountered the burning bush. The Samaritan woman was drawing water from the well, as she must have done every day, when Jesus met her and offered her living water.

In this season, God reminds us that each moment holds the possibility of encountering the sacred. It is those seemingly ordinary moments which make up our days, and, as Annie Dillard writes, "How we spend our days is, after all, how we spend our lives."

Now it is nighttime. I have completed most of my nightly rituals, including the reading that helps me settle into the slumbering hours. Tonight it was a portion of Hannah Hinchman's *A Trail through Leaves,* a delicious volume I found last summer and finally am savoring in this season. Getting up to turn off the light, I gaze about my room. My eyes take in the stacks of books and papers that the floor around my bed draws like a magnet. There's a collection of poems by Rumi, a book of essays by Audre Lorde, a stack of magazines that arrived from Sandra in today's mail, a copy of Marjorie Kinnan Rawlings's *Cross Creek* that my boyfriend and I are reading to each other. In the corner sits a deep set of shelves that he and I built not long ago so that I could move my art paper from beneath my futon to a more accessible place. A pair of jeans lies across the back of my drafting chair, tossed there earlier tonight after I returned from an evening of acoustic music at the nearby bookstore. A new oil lamp sits on the cedar table, a gift from a friend's recent trip to New Orleans. My cat Zeke lies under the table, his paws tucked under himself, settled in for the night or at least until he jumps onto my futon during the dark hours.

Turning off the light, I think of how it is the ordinary that roots me. And it is there that God challenges us to unmask her, begs us to unveil him. Night into day into night, in the crevices of the familiar, in the rhythms of our daily rituals and habits and encounters, God beckons us like Wisdom calling her followers daily to her gates.

*Attention consists of suspending our thought, leaving it*

*detached, empty, and ready to be penetrated by the object.*

—SIMONE WEIL, *WAITING FOR GOD*

*I am inside your looking.*

—RUMI, "NO ROOM FOR FORM," *THE ESSENTIAL RUMI*

uring the year I lived at San Pedro, I went almost every day to the small dock outside my cabin. Walking out onto the narrow boards, I would stand and wait. Scanning the shoreline, eyeing the water, I was practicing my latest lesson: learning to see.

In her book *Pilgrim at Tinker Creek,* Annie Dillard writes of reading Marius von Senden's book *Space and Sight,* in which he describes the time when surgeons discovered how to successfully remove cataracts. They fanned out across the United States and Europe performing operations, many of them on patients who had lived with blindness since birth. The surgeons' case reports described the terror that sometimes ensued. The patients blind since birth had not developed the necessary pathways between eyes and brain; their eyes could register images, but their brains couldn't make sense of them. They had never learned to see. Some longed to return to their familiar world; others set about learning to navigate in their new one.

Annie writes of one man who "practiced his vision" by taking one of his boots, throwing it a distance, and trying to gauge how far away it was. Throw by throw, boot by boot, the man worked to gain a sense of perspective.

Reading these stories, I began to understand seeing as a process, something that is not a given even for people whose eyes have always worked. I miss thousands of details a day, overlooking the God who dwells in the commonplace, passing by the smoldering bush that might have burst into flame had I gazed on it long enough. So I would go out on the dock, hoping to learn. I stayed until I saw something I might otherwise have missed. It was often just as I turned to go, thinking there was nothing new under the San Pedro sun, that my unseeing would begin to erode. Finally I would notice the reeds giving way to a great blue heron, the ripple in the water that turned into the back of an alligator, the shadows in the trees that revealed themselves as cormorants settling in for the evening.

Inhabit these glances,
God of my eyes.
Dwell in my gazing,
and in the line of my sight
make your home.
Let the force of my looking
lay bare the ways you hide
your spirit in the shadows,
your laughter on the wing.

As I did the artwork that accompanies the introduction to this section, I began to think about the ways we perceive. I thought about how God offers the world not only to our eyes but to all our senses, and how those senses can serve as doorways to wisdom. In the midst of those thoughts, I returned to Carter Heyward's book *Touching Our Strength*. I came across these words: "If we learn to trust our senses, our capacities to touch, taste, smell, hear, see, and thereby know, they can teach us what is good and what is bad, what is real and what is false, for us in relation to one another and to the earth and cosmos."

God of eye and ear,
of taste and touch,
of smell and of every sense
and source of knowing,
bless me not
with sight alone
but bless me also
with ears to hear
your voice
and tongue to taste
your essence
and nose to breathe
your fragrance
and fingertips to touch
your nearness
and heart to open
that door
which is wisdom,
which is wonder,
which is all.

n the day before I moved out of the parsonage in which I had lived during my ministry at St. Luke's, I received a phone call from a pastor in Pennsylvania inviting me to speak at a retreat the following spring. "We're thinking of doing something on the theme of women and change," she said. "Would you be interested?" I laughed, telling her that she had found me in the midst of packing up my house and that I thought I could find something to say about women and change.

This image emerged as I thought about the upcoming retreat and about the changes that had taken place in my own life. As I worked at my drafting table, I thought, too, of the Navajo legend of Changing Woman. Daughter of Earth and Sky, raised by First Man and First Woman, she is the creator of the Navajo people. Renewing her youth as the seasons unfold, she does not fear change but draws on its power as it cycles within her.

Many seasons have passed as I have worked on this book, and I finally feel that my soul has mostly caught up with the deep changes presented by these seasons. I have navigated the risks posed by moving into a ministry beyond the local church and have settled well into the rhythms of this new life. After a year of living in the cabin at San Pedro, I moved into a nearby garage apartment. Paul and I are no longer together, having stopped dating right before I moved during the summer. In the autumn I entered a new relationship—with a man also, somewhat confusingly, named Paul—and I continue to marvel at the wonder and challenge of sharing the path together.

In her book *The Mother's Songs,* Meinrad Craighead writes, "Revolving at her own center, Changing Woman unwinds the incalculable curvatures of time, calling the minutes and months, naming the seasons and years to measure her turnings. Her unity is

perceptible in the two moving points of our own spiral dance in time: the journey evolving outward, the search involving inward." I think of an image from a postcard which Elizabeth Johnson includes in her book *She Who Is.* The picture depicts a Mexican woman spinning cotton into thread. On the back of the postcard, the sender wrote, "This is a wonderful image of God, no? I think we are neither in the raw cotton or the thread, but in the twirling. . . ."

And so we twirl in the spiraling seasons, held by the God who is nexus and source and who roots us in the midst of all our changes.

In my turning
and returning,
take me in
and let me go.

At the center
of the spinning,
root me deep
and set me loose.

At the still point
of the spiral,
draw me close
and send me forth.

In the passage
of the seasons,
hold me fast
and set me free.

# SUMMER SOLSTICE

**M**y new home is one large room situated over a two-car garage. It's even smaller than the cabin I lived in at San Pedro, but it affords certain delights. A window at the top of my stairs offers access to the roof, where I can sit on sunny days or share a cup of tea with a friend on warm, starry nights. Dwelling on the second story, I can peer straight into the tops of the trees outside my large windows. And though the refrigerator in the efficiency kitchen barely comes to my knees, the bathtub on the other side of the wall offers opportunities for long soaks that the large but tubless shower in the cabin couldn't provide.

What makes the most difference in this space, however, are two skylights that grace the ceiling. They provide so much light that I turn on few, if any, lamps during the day. With one of the skylights situated above my drafting table, the brightness is an artist's dream. I who love shadows and the nighttime hours have found myself enchanted by the light.

My soul has shifted with the lengthening light, tilting toward the sun as the earth does on its path toward the summer solstice. The shadows are still there and will lengthen in their turn, but for now sunlight is the host, bidding me to discover what dwells in this bright season.

Brother Sun,
I greet you,
companion of my day.

You are icon
of the burning God.
You are creature
of her blazing hand.
You are messenger
of her flaming love.
You are child
of her scorching fire.

I offer you
my shadows.
I turn my face to you
like every greening thing.

Search me with your fervent hand,
hold me in your fevered gaze,
that I may blaze and yet not be consumed,
thou burning fire,
thou Brother Sun.

BROTHER SUN

oonlight, too, sometimes streams through the sky-
lights. The first time I saw it visit my room, I had
just turned off the lamp by my bed. Drawing my cov-
ers over me, I noticed a pool of silver on the floor. I rose and looked
through the skylight to see a nearly full moon. Standing in its light,
I remembered my friend Carolyn telling me of how, as a child, she
would lie on her bed in any position that would allow her to receive
the touch of the moonlight coming through her window. This moonlight, shy on its first visit, didn't reach my bed, but it traced a path
along the floor while I slept, marking time as the hours passed.

Sister Moon,
I greet you,
companion of my darkness.

You are icon
of the fluid God.
Waxing to your fullness,
you do not explode;
waning to your emptiness,
you do not die.
Through all your changes
you give your radiance.
You embrace your shadows
and are born again.

From the burning day
I hide in you.
In the darkening night
I seek your face.

Guard me in my restless dreams,
bless me with your ebb and flow
that I may weather every change,
thou vigil light,
thou Sister Moon.

SISTER MOON

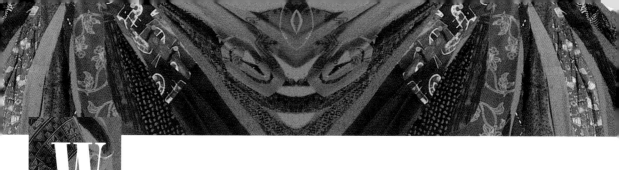

When I was growing up, both my sets of grandparents had summer homes next to each other on a lake. I spent much of my summers running back and forth, barefoot and swimsuit-clad, between the two houses. One of the most comforting sounds lodged in my memory is that of the waves lapping against the shore at night. Stealing through the open windows of the room where my sister and I slept with white cotton sheets and yellow chenille bedspreads tangled around our legs, the sound of lapping water worked itself into the rhythm of our summer slumber.

When I moved to San Pedro, to my cabin beside its lake, I had a sense of return. I couldn't hear the water at night; the reeds at the lake's edge absorbed its lapping before it reached the shore. Still, I knew it lay just beyond my window, waiting.

One of the recurring images in the Bible is of the God who provides water in the wilderness. To the wandering Israelites, to a devastated Hagar with her dying son, to the Samaritan woman at the well, God gives wellsprings of life and hope.

As a child dreaming by the lake, I didn't know about wilderness, but I do now. I know how one can become thirsty beyond measure and hardly realize it till one has been brought to the water again. I know the shock that comes with sudden quenching, with drenching that leaves us wondering how we ever did without.

God of the waters,
help me to know
that there will be wilderness,
but the wilderness
will turn to green land;
that there will be desert,
but in the desert
a spring;
that in the heart
of the rock
of my life
will begin to flow
a river
washing through
the chasm of my soul;
and that I will walk
wet with memory
when again I touch
dry land.

*Wisdom is a tree of life for those who hold her fast;*

*those who cling to her live happy lives.*

O n the top of the bookcase beside my desk sit wood carvings of a bear and two birds, their burnished planes catching the shifting light. Gifts from Paul—the first Paul—during the time we dated, they are the stunning work of his own hands. Paul is a woodcarver. He uses only pieces of wood that others have passed on to him, choosing the best ones to shape and sand until a form emerges that fairly breathes with life. He can see deep into the wood, and he knows by name nearly everything that comes to him: English walnut, mahogany, oak, cherry. . . From him I learned about spalted wood, a partially rotten wood that comes from such trees as pecan, beech, and maple. The decay gives a stunning effect when carved. From Paul I also learned how zebra wood, named for its dark stripes, smells absolutely foul but contains a gorgeous grain.

In the Welsh language, the words for *wood* and *wisdom* are similar, perhaps owing to the ancient Druids who worshiped in sacred groves of trees. Listening to Paul talk about wood, I know I am listening to someone who still offers it a certain reverence, who perceives the spirit it houses. Paul is one of the most grounded people I know. I think it must be the trees in his bones.

Creating God,
for those who are wise
to the ways of your earth:
thank you.

For those who listen
to the language
of tree, rock,
river, earth,
ocean, stars,
creatures, sky:
praise.

Teach us
the vocabulary
to convey our care,
the words to tell the earth
we hear her crying for peace,
the syllables of solace
for all we have lost,
the gestures of healing
for all we have harmed.

Once upon a time, construction paper was pretty much the only kind of art paper I knew about. I fashioned my first serious collages from cheap construction paper I'd had lying around for years. When I started using origami paper, which provided intense, solid colors, I thought I was really moving up in the world. My next big step came in using some wonderfully textured wrapping paper I had stumbled upon in an Atlanta store. Then I learned to scour clothing catalogs for the wonderful colors and patterns I found there.

I vividly recall the first time I walked into a store dedicated to fine papers. The first time I visited Toronto after my sister and her family moved there, I called the local art college to ask where I could find an art supply store with a good stock of paper. They directed me to The Japanese Paper Place. I hesitated, associating Japanese paper with a quite thin, delicate sort of paper that I rarely use in my work. Upon walking in, however, I was transported to a wondrous new world. Stocking papers not only from Asia but from around the world, the store provided a dazzling display of textures, colors, and patterns. I was in paper paradise.

During my first visit I was still living by the philosophy that I only bought paper that I knew how I would use. By the time I went back the next year, I had, thankfully, learned to buy paper just because I liked it, trusting that its purpose would eventually emerge. I came home laden with six large mailing tubes of paper, filled with exquisite sheets bearing names that read like a litany: *momi irobiki, crepe, kensha, kinwashi, raddish, sugikawa, sunago mingei, chiri kyoseishi, lokta.* I bought corn paper made by a women's collective in Central America, paper made from thinly sliced cork, and bark paper fashioned in a way that did not destroy the trees.

kinwashi

SUZUKAWA

I am rich in paper, delighting in the colors and textures that slowly are making their way into artwork. I believe God dwells in those papers, resides in the process of transformation by which trees and bark and corn and papyrus and all manner of plants give way to pulp, then beautiful sheets of paper. I grieve for the indiscriminate, unreplenished use of vast swaths of trees for the mass production of paper—paper that I know contributes to my own survival as a writer, artist, and voracious reader. I celebrate the farmers and foresters who take care with their growing and harvesting, the artisans who acknowledge the life that has flowed through the fibers they transform, the spirits that still sing as the colors and textures become designs and patterns at the altar of my drafting table.

May I feel you
beneath my fingers,
the landscape of your
smooth, tough,
slick, coarse,
fine, textured surface
awakening my skin;
your colors of
sky, sun,
rivers, earth,
blood, marrow
beckoning my eye.
Let the piecing of these patterns
mend this torn and tattered soul;
let this layering of papers
be a prayer for making whole.

*Jesus told them another parable: "The kingdom of heaven is like yeast that a woman took and mixed in with three measures of flour until all of it was leavened."*

—MATTHEW 13:33

O n Tuesdays, David bakes bread. Not just a few loaves: thirty or forty is usual for a bread day. When I lived at San Pedro, sometimes I would walk up the road to the kitchen and sit as he worked. Usually I liked to go toward the end of the afternoon, while the bread baked in the ovens and the incredible smell greeted me before I'd gotten all the way inside. But sometimes I would go on the earlier end of the day, while the bread was still in the works. I remember discovering how wonderfully therapeutic it is to punch down big, fat mounds of dough. And I remember a day when David invited me to help him knead and shape the bread. I could never quite get my thumbs to work the kind of nimble magic on the dough that his did, but it was like being invited into the holy of holies to work on David's bread. People for miles around know about his bread, and they'll come a distance for it. When the bread is finished, he lays the golden loaves on the kitchen counter in the guest house and leaves them for the people who will stop by. They'll come in, select their loaves, and leave a donation in the box. The money that's left after expenses will go toward the farmworker community in Apopka. And anyone who eats David's bread will not go to bed hungry that night.

Pondering Jesus' comments about the kingdom of God, I think he must have watched somebody making bread, too. Most likely it was his mother Mary he watched as she took the yeast and mixed it into the flour and stirred in the oil and the salt and worked the dough and baked it and fed the steaming loaf to the hungry Jesus. Perhaps it was just this sort of memory that helped him understand and explain what the kingdom of God is like: that it comes not with thunderbolts but that it rises in small ways, like a mustard seed sown in a field, growing with rain and sun and care to become a huge shrub. Or like the making of bread, with God working as a bakerwoman to take the yeast, to leaven the flour, to work the dough, to wait for the rising, to bake it and break it and bless it and share it so that those who eat of it will not be hungry.

—FROM "CREATIVE LOAFING," A SERMON I PREACHED DURING
WOMEN'S WEEK AT CANDLER SCHOOL OF THEOLOGY, OCTOBER 1998

Only this:
that I may never hunger
for that
which is not
your bread.

The recent news of the marriage of an old love sent me into several days of deep pondering. It happens periodically that the choices I have made rear their heads and demand to know if I still think I chose rightly. This time I thought back to a trip I made to Atlanta during the autumn after I moved to San Pedro, ostensibly to do some research for this book in the theology library. Digging back into the journal I carried with me during that trip, I found these words: *I am sitting outside in the Cannon Chapel/Bishops Hall courtyard. It is absolutely gorgeous today. Cool weather but sunny and blue blue blue sky. I've kicked off my shoes and am sitting in the sun. I've had a feeling that this trip to Atlanta is only partly about doing research. I think there were a variety of reasons for coming here, and at least some of them had to do with perspective. It seemed important to come here at this point of transition in my life. And to be here and know that I have made some excellent choices. That I can hardly imagine doing anything else with my life.*

In Isak Dinesen's novel *Babette's Feast*, later made into a stunning movie, a powerful scene unfolds toward the end. To the feast which Babette prepares for the elderly sisters who helped rescue her years before, a general comes. As a young man he had fallen in love with one of the sisters, whom the father, leader of a strict religious sect, kept closely guarded. Moved by the remarkable feast and by this meeting that has taken place nearly a lifetime later, the general stands to raise a toast. He speaks of the choices we make in life and of coming to realize that everything returns to us, even that which we, in our choosing, had to leave behind. I'm not sure about that; the mystic in me believes in the final unity of all things, but the pragmatist in me believes that the choices we make mean that certain lives are forever lost to us. Yet I carry the words he speaks: "We tremble before making our choice in life, and after having made it, again tremble in fear of having chosen wrong. But the moment comes when our eyes are opened, and we see and realize that grace is infinite."

Sitting in my room, windows open to a cool day that feels much like that one in Atlanta, I think of the choices I have made. Most of them, the big ones, I would make again. I don't know how or whether what I left behind will return to me, save in the guise of questions about whether I chose rightly. But in the unfolding of these days I gather to myself the grace, the infinite grace, that has come in the choices made along this spiraling path.

Thou who dwells at the crossroads,
bless the choices gone before,
the roads not taken,
the thresholds not crossed,
the lives not lived.
On the terrain that we have chosen
may we travel lightly,
shed of regrets
and shorn of illusions
of other landscapes
that we reckoned
and did not choose to cross.

ome of my most sacred moments have unfolded in the sharing of tea. With our heads bent over steaming cups, time slows and shifts, opening spaces for words that might get squelched in racing minutes during the rest of the day. Silence, too, broods over the brew, and the quiet enters us as the tea's flavor enters the water in which it steeps.

When Brenda, Debby, Alice, and I traveled to New Zealand, we spent several nights at a wondrous bed and breakfast in Christchurch. Each morning we sat down to a table laden with a dazzling array of food. Bea, our hostess at the Cashmere House, filled our cups with a heavenly-smelling fruit tea. After finding out what kind of tea it was, I went to a market and purchased several boxes to stash in my suitcase for the trip home. I have yet to find anything like it in this country and was sorry when a friend and I finished the last box.

I saved the boxes, though, and pulled them out when I began to work on this image. As I cut into the first box to make the border (and the woman's irises), I could still smell the tea that it had contained. I could smell all the way back to the table that Bea had set for us, pouring our daily tea into our waiting cups, beckoning us to savor all that lay before us.

I would take
and drink of you,
Vessel of mystery,
bearing within you
potent depths,
containing within you
what quenches
and quickens:

to my sorrow
you offer soothing;
to my despair
you offer desire;
to my complacence,
your challenge;
to my resistance,
your rest.

Be well assured
I am not lulled by you.
There is a bite to your brew
that sets me forever on edge,
a taste that leaves me never slaked;
but with mouth trembling
and thirsty,
I would take
and drink of you.

In the course of experiencing and pondering the turning of seasons, I have come to recognize that particular times of the year hold special power and intrigue for me. Like the lines of energy that some suppose to run through the earth, concentrating at sacred sites, the spiraling seasons contain an energy that intensifies for me at particular times. The trinity of days at the end of October and beginning of November mark such a time: Halloween, the Feast of All Saints, and the Feast of All Souls inevitably herald some sort of turning as the year draws to its end. Why these days hold such power for me, I'm not sure; whether it's because they occur in the unfolding of fall, my favorite season, or because long-ago ancestors celebrated these holy days or simply because they capture my imagination, I don't know. But I have learned that it pays to be attentive to what unfolds in this trio of days.

In the ancient Celtic tradition, the festival of Samhain fell around November 1 and marked the turning of the year from summer to winter. The ancient Celts believed that at this turning, the gates between this world and the otherworld of the dead swung open, allowing for contact between the living and those who had gone before. After the rise of Christianity, this festival became known as the Feast of All Saints or the Feast of All Hallows, during which prayers were said for the faithful departed. Many of the traditions of the old Samhain festival, however, lingered in celebrations held the day before All Saints: October 31, known as All Hallows' Eve or Halloween. The Feast of All Souls, celebrated on November 2, became a time to pray for the souls of all departed Christians, including those believed to be in Purgatory.

Keeper of the Gate,
guard me on this threshold;

Keeper of the Threshold,
guard me at this door;

Keeper of the Door,
guard me in this passage;

thou path in whom I journey,
guard me evermore.

# ALL HALLOWS' EVE
## (October 31)

Halloween begins this year in Paul's kitchen, where we talk as we slice vegetables for our supper. Later, as the vegetables roast in the oven and soup simmers on the stove, we dance in the living room, moving with the turning season. It is the latest in the series of moments that I have come to share with him: cooking, eating, sharing tea, reading to one another, going for walks with his elegant whippet named Ashley, talking, not talking. I love the sheer ordinariness of it all, the rhythm of days that we have discovered with one another.

Some say the veil between this world and the next is very thin on this night, and I imagine others at the table where we sit when our meal is finally ready. I think of those who journey now with the knowledge of how utterly precious each moment is, who know that what we carry with us to meet them will not be the money we made or the possessions we gathered or the jobs we slaved over. It will be this: how we lingered with one another, how we tended the bonds between us, how we walked upon the earth, how we savored the rare and wondrous gift given to us.

## Gesture

There is a certain way
that I touch my face
and he is suddenly there.
The fingers falling across my cheek
are my grandfather's,
the gesture
a point of meeting,
a peering through the veil,
his touch telling me
to love this flesh
that flows with the blood
from our common well.

## the veil is very thin

# Feast of All Saints

**B**renda, Debby, Alice, and I landed in Christchurch, New Zealand, on November 1. We had completely missed Halloween; we left Orlando on October 30 and passed it somewhere in the air as we winged our way through many time zones. We arrived sleepy and bleary-eyed after nearly twenty-four hours of travel, which included sharing a plane with Queen Elizabeth from Los Angeles to Auckland, New Zealand. We never saw her, though we have complimentary pens, menus, and stationery emblazoned with the words "The Royal Flight."

I thought that in a city named Christchurch we would surely find at least one church celebrating the holy day. Our hosts at the bed and breakfast located an Anglican congregation holding a special service, and after letting us lose ourselves in slumber for several hours, Monty drove us, with breathtaking speed, down the hill into the city and dropped us off at the church. I remember little of the service, but the smell of incense settled deep into my memory.

As we remembered those who had died, I thought of my friend Edward, whose ashes now rest at a church called All Saints'. Several months after his death, I spent the night in the home he had shared with Ray. During the dark night, I dreamed of Edward. We talked again, each of us knowing he had died, yet somehow conversing in that netherworld of dreams where encounters happen beyond the bounds of time and logic. Waking beneath my heavy quilt the next morning, I remembered Edward's palpable presence during the night, then walked upstairs to the rooms still heavy with his absence.

124

In
Wisdom's
Path

*Ordinary Time*

For those
who walked with us,
this is a prayer.

For those
who have gone ahead,
this is a blessing.

For those
who touched and tended us,
who lingered with us
while they lived,
this is a thanksgiving.

For those
who journey still with us
in the shadows of awareness,
in the crevices of memory,
in the landscape of our dreams,
this is a benediction.

# FEAST OF ALL SOULS

## (November 2)

During the year that I lived at San Pedro, this trio of holy days fell during our annual Audire instructional weekend. We spent the weekend studying mysticism, looking particularly at the Spanish mystics St. Teresa of Avila and St. John of the Cross. I begrudged spending this particular weekend on retreat but decided that spending it in the company of the mystics could prove interesting.

I went into the weekend weary, feeling tender and exposed. I had spent a great deal of effort in recent days on conversations I needed to have, seeking to dispel the silences that had knotted up in my throat. My throat throbbed with the energy of words said and unsaid.

On the eve of All Souls, coming back to my cabin early from the festivities the staff of Audire had planned for the holy day, I shed my clothes and climbed into the shower. I placed a candle in the dark window and let the hot water wash over me. Touching my hand to the wet skin stretched across my throat, I felt a cry wrench itself from deep inside me. It was as if something had burst, as if that touch had let loose all the silences within me, and I stood wailing as the water rushed over me.

I didn't understand quite what was happening, but on this eve of All Souls, I sensed that the ghosts I carried within me were seeking their freedom. The silences I had allowed myself to keep, the grief to which I struggled to give voice: they gave themselves to the water, to the flow that washed over me in the turning of the season.

When I walk
in the company of ghosts,
O God,
watch over me.

When I am visited
by half-healed wounds,
by unnamed sorrows,
by unvoiced anger;
when dreams bring the ache
I was determined to forget
and the shadows of passions lost
come to call,
keep me in your gaze.

Teach me the words
that will appease them,
the charms
that will release them,
the blessings
that will give them solace
and send them on their way.

Keep me,
O God,
when I am growing weary
and walking
in the company of ghosts.

uring our visit with my family in Gainesville over Thanksgiving, Paul came down with a terrible cold. Despite a trip to a clinic on Thanksgiving morning, the cold worsened, deepening his cough and causing high fevers at night. When we returned to Orlando, I urged him to see another doctor. Taking some cough medicine by his house the night before his appointment, I was alarmed by his persistent fever and racking cough. "I'm not leaving," I told him, and through most of the night I sat with him, laying cool washcloths on his forehead, bringing him drinks and aspirin, holding him as the deep coughing shook his body. *How can he possibly have anything left inside him to cough up?* I thought after hours had passed. Soon the doctor would confirm what I had begun to suspect: Paul had pneumonia.

In the long hours of that night, I thought of friends of mine who had provided care for loved ones with serious, long-term illnesses. I marveled at those who have found the courage and grace to journey with a companion whose world has shifted radically due to injury or illness. I have heard them speak of how what is ordinary changes, how the accoutrements and logistics of injury or illness become part of the intricate weave of daily life.

In her remarkable book *Ordinary Time,* Nancy Mairs writes of how she signed the contract for that book after her husband began chemotherapy to treat a large, malignant tumor in his intestine. "If God is going to be present to me," Nancy recalls thinking one evening as she tended George while he retched into the pink plastic basin they had brought home with them from the hospital, "she'll simply have to wade through the mess chemotherapy is currently making in our lives. I can't scramble away from it up to some loftier plane."

God of those who suffer,
you wore our flesh,
and in the terror of the cross
you wore the outrage of our pain.
You know the intimacies of this flesh,
the intricacies of illness,
and in our fragile bodies
you make your dwelling place.

May those who live in pain
know you
breathing into every ache,
weeping into every wound,
dwelling in every hurt.

May those who live
at the limits of endurance
be met with the tenderness
of your touch,
and may your garments of resurrection
enfold those who dwell
at the threshold of despair.

Bless this flesh,
this aching, hopeful,
wearied, wondering flesh
where you make your home.
In this temple of your spirit,
sing the song of transformation
that will lead us to your waters,
that will make these dry bones dance.

O ver the past few years I have become enchanted by the work of the painter Daniel Nevins. With an air of folklore and myth, his paintings capture moments of stillness in hinted-at unfolding stories: a boy daydreams in the top of a tree; a couple lie together in a field at the water's edge; a girl stands motionless in a stream, clutching the folds of her dress. The images stir my memory, both with their content and with the way that Daniel layers each painting; the surface seems, as one critic has noted, to possess a memory of its own.

On a trip to Asheville last fall, I met Daniel for lunch at a downtown café. I had never seen him before, but I was struck by a sense of recognition as we talked over our meal. As with his paintings, Daniel's spirit felt familiar to me, and I was not surprised to discover that we had drunk from some of the same wells.

After lunch we went to his studio, where for the first time I saw originals of his work. He paints on large surfaces of wood, and standing close enough to see the details firsthand was remarkable. One recently finished painting, titled "Whoever Brought Me Here Will Have to Take Me Home," drew its name from a line of a Rumi poem. Later I went back to my copy of *The Essential Rumi* to find that poem. The translator, Coleman Barks, titles the first chapter after that line and goes on to observe, "The Qur'an says, 'We are all returning.' "

Reading the poem, I thought of the steps on my own journey of return: this layering of bits of colored paper onto the page, this restless searching for words, this lighting a candle in the night and listening, this touching my beloved's face, this standing in a sunlit studio with one who speaks a kindred language, this eating sleeping dreaming longing pulling me, beckoning me, drawing me home.

# For Daniel Standing in His Studio
## and Contemplating the Frame

I left the studio
with a score of unasked questions,
and if I knew what they were,
I would write them here
and here.
As it is, I'm still working my way
toward the language,
toward some syllables to fill the space
between the intake of breath
at the beginning of a sentence
and the rise in pitch at the end
that signals a question.

What I know is this:
there are words with bloody fingerprints
that I have tried to hang onto,
and some that have served me well.
In the swirl of images
visiting me these days,

they are looking for a place to settle,
a space from which to describe
the lay of this shifting land.

I think you have some wisdom
about weathering the storm,
about giving yourself to the vortex
that takes us where vocabulary
hesitates to go.

And if I ever think of the questions,
perhaps I'll simply
tear them into shreds,
turn them into pictures
for you who knows
darkness as a path,
painting as a prayer,
art as a wrestled blessing
on this journey of return.

Wisdom has built her house, she has hewn her seven pillars.

She has slaughtered her animals, she has mixed her wine, she has also

set her table. She has sent out her servant girls, she calls from the

highest places in town, "You that are simple, turn in here!"

To those without sense she says, "Come, eat of my bread and drink of

the wine I have mixed. Lay aside immaturity, and live,

and walk in the way of insight."

—PROVERBS 9:1–6

*A*re these people you know?" a friend asked when she saw this picture. Yes and no. When I first began working on this, I wanted to set the table with famil- iar faces. But with only thirteen places, how could I choose? The guest list for my dream feast would be enormously long, more than one table could hold. I didn't want to leave anyone out.

Yet these folks, Wisdom's dinner guests, are familiar to me. The spirits and some of the physical features of people who have shared my journey found their way into this piece. The figures evoke various family members, friends, and companions, those known to me as well as those I hope to cross paths with one day.

As I worked on this piece, I was visited by memories of wise companions and of tables we have shared. In this spiraling journey, one of the gifts that has sustained me most has been the breaking of bread, the opportunity to linger over the table with folks who have accompanied me along the way. I made this for two friends in particular who have taught me a great deal about feasting. They have shown me, again and again, that where there is bread and wine and friendship, there is holy ground.

To your table
you bid us come.
You have set the places,
you have poured the wine,
and there is always room,
you say,
for one more.

And so we come.
From the streets
and from the alleys
we come.

From the deserts
and from the hills
we come.

From the ravages of poverty
and from the palaces of privilege
we come.

Running,
limping,
carried,
we come.

We are bloodied with our wars,
we are wearied with our wounds,
we carry our dead within us,
and we reckon with their ghosts.

We hold the seeds of healing,
we dream of a new creation,
we know the things
that make for peace,
and we struggle
to give them wings.

And yet, to your table
we come.
Hungering for your bread,
we come;
thirsting for your wine,
we come;
singing your song
in every language,
speaking your name
in every tongue,
in conflict and in communion,
in discord and in desire,
we come,
O God of Wisdom,
we come.

Page xi: In addition to providing their own pro-
gramming, the San Pedro Center welcomes
groups and individuals seeking a place of quiet
retreat. For more information, contact San Pedro
at 2400 Dike Rd., Winter Park, FL 32792;
407-671-6322; e-mail: SPCDove@aol.com.

Page xiii: For more on the Re-Imagining
Conference, see *Re-Membering and Re-Imagining*,
edited by Nancy J. Berneking and Pamela Carter
Joern (Cleveland: The Pilgrim Press, 1995).

Page 15: For information or to subscribe to *The
Other Side* magazine, contact them at 1-800-700-
9280; 300 W. Apsley St., Philadelphia, PA 19144;
www.theotherside.org.

Page 23: Marketplace and Ten Thousand Villages
are organizations that equitably foster and market
the work of artisans from such places as Latin
America and India. In addition to providing fair
wages, these organizations often provide training
and other forms of creative aid to the artisans.
Catalogs containing beautiful clothing, house-
wares, and gifts can be obtained from each organization in the following ways:

Marketplace: Handwork of India: 1455 Ashland
Ave., Evanston, IL 60201-4001; 1-800-726-
8905; www.marketplaceindia.com.
Ten Thousand Villages: 704 Main St., P.O. Box
500, Akron, PA 17501-0500; 717-859-8100;
www.villages.ca.

Alternatives for Simple Living, also known (simply!) as Alternatives, describes itself as "a nonprofit organization that equips people of faith to
challenge consumerism, live justly and celebrate
responsibly. Started in 1973 as a protest against
the commercialization of Christmas, our focus is
on encouraging celebrations that reflect conscien-
tious ways of living." They publish a catalog containing books and other resources. You can reach
them at P.O. Box 2857, Sioux City, IA 51106; 1-
800-821-6153; www.simpleliving.org. One of the
great books they carry is *Unplug the Christmas
Machine: A Complete Guide to Putting Love and
Joy Back into the Season*, by Jo Robinson and Jean
Coppock Staeheli (New York: Quill 1991).

Also check out these folks:

SERRV International, a nonprofit program that
promotes social and economic progress of artisans
in developing regions. 500 Main St., New
Windsor, MD 21776-0365; 1-800-422-5915;
www. serrv.org.

Syracuse Cultural Workers, an educational and
cultural organization devoted to inspiring and fos-
tering justice, equality, and freedom through creative expression; they publish a fabulous catalog
which includes seasonal greeting cards as well as
posters, T-shirts, and books. P.O. Box 6367,
Syracuse, NY 13217; 315-474-1132; www.syrcul-
turalworkers.org.

Page 46: Sources for information on St. Brigid
include the following:

Carmichael, Alexander. *Carmina Gadelica.* Edited
by C J Moore. Hudson, NY: Lindisfarne Press,
1992. See especially Carmichael's notes to no.
70, "Genealogy of Bride," 580–86.
Matthews, Caitlin. *The Celtic Book of Days.*
Rochester, VT.: Destiny Books, 1995.
Sellner, Edward C. "Brigit of Kildare, Golden
Sparkling Flame: A Study in the Liminality of
Women's Spiritual Power." *Vox Benedictina*, vol.
11, 1994.

Page 61: In various countries in Central and South
America, women whose family members have
been kidnapped, imprisoned, and often tortured
and killed by government soldiers have come to
be known as the Mothers of the Disappeared. At
the risk of their own lives, many of the women
have banded together to seek justice and information about their *desaparecidos.* For a moving
account of one such group, the Mothers of the
Plaza de Mayo in Argentina, see Jo Fisher's book
*Mothers of the Disappeared* (Boston: South End
Press, 1989).

Page 117: When in Toronto, visit The Japanese
Paper Place at 887 Queen St. W. (416-703-
0089). A pleasant, if less tactilely satisfying, experience can be had by visiting their Web site at
www.interlog.com/~washi.

Page 129: This artwork was created for Holy
Ground, a dynamic ministry based in Asheville,
North Carolina, which offers learning experiences, retreat opportunities, and times of worship
designed "to empower all persons to live more
justly and more fully in love with God, each
other, the earth, and themselves." Based on
Christian feminist practices, Holy Ground also
draws from the wisdom of other faith traditions.
For more information, contact Holy Ground at
P.O. Box 8512, Asheville, NC 28814; 828-236-
0222; e-mail: HolyGrnd@aol.com.